TEA

Roland Gööck

with 50 recipes
from around the world,
and exclusive photographs by
Hans Joachim Döbbelin

SIGLOCH
EDITION

Right: "Abwarten und Tee trinken" is a saying from East Prussia which literally means "Drink tea while you wait" but is often translated by the English phrase "Wait and see". Whichever version you prefer, both accurately portray the calmness and hospitality of the Moroccans and give an indication of just what makes tea so different from any other drink – the solemn reverence with which tea has come to be regarded over thousands of years, and its rituals which are unknown anywhere else in the history of drink. According to the Japanese tea sage Kakuzo Okakura, tea "possesses a delicate magic which makes it irresistible and open to idealisation". Tea is "the drink of the sages, of contemplation, patience and sensitivity; it is the drink of those who can quietly smile at themselves and who can disregard life's imperfections with an ironic smile".

Translation by Pholiota Translations, London (Simon Morgan, Daniel Bird)

© 1990 Sigloch Edition, Zeppelinstrasse 35a, D-7118 Künzelsau
Sigloch Edition & Co., Lettenstrasse 3, CH-6343 Rotkreuz
Publisher: Hans Kalis
Reproduction prohibited. All rights reserved. Printed in Germany
Editing and Production: Friedhelm Messow and Michael Sanny,
Sigloch Edition, Künzelsau
Reproduction: PHG Lithos, Martinsried
Typesetting: Setzerei Lihs, Ludwigsburg
Printing: Graphische Betriebe Eberl, Immenstadt
Paper: 135 g/m² paper BVS from Papierfabrik Scheufelen, Lenningen
Binding: Sigloch Buchbinderei, Künzelsau
ISBN 3-89393-023-X

5000 Years of Tea History

It is estimated today that both green tea and the later black tea have been known throughout Asia for over five thousand years, and that they have been used for the past three thousand years as a ritual and a cultural drink. Experts still cannot agree on where tea actually originated from – did it come from the highlands of south-western China, northern Burma or eastern India, or did it spread from Assam in India outwards to China? "There are three elements which combine to create the unique fascination of tea," the German office for tea in Hamburg explains: "Firstly, its restorative effect, which aids concentration and stimulates the drinker without agitating him. Then there is the calming and soothing effect it has on the stomach and the digestive system. And finally, there is the unique and rich aroma, peculiar to each particular tea type and method of preparation."

After water, tea is the most popular drink in the world: "No other plant wields so much influence over social life", it is claimed in a reference book from the turn of the century. "Tea is a despot in Asia; and Europe and America willingly offer their taxes to it. One nation after another nestles under its gentle yoke."

The tea-house in China has the same importance for the Chinese as the pub has for the Europeans. Guests there can choose from twenty different types of tea.

Tea in China – Myth, Legend and Conjecture

Only the Chinese can say with any accuracy who it was who "invented" tea – their Emperor Shen Nung who resided in the Hunan province, south of the Yellow River. According to Chinese legend, he had the body of a snake and the head of a man, though other sources attribute to him the body of a man and the head of an ox. He was one of the "Three Exalted Ones", the founders of all arts and crafts. Shen Nung was the first to concern himself with tilling the soil and for this reason he is named in history as the "Farmer God". In addition to this, he wrote a book of medicine containing numerous recipes such as one for a pill of immortality, and one for making gold. He was less popular as the "God of the Hot Wind", for in this role he would dry out the earth in the fields. The intervention of Ch'ih Sung-tzu, the "God of Rain", would be the reason for good harvests, if Shen Nung blew one hot wind too many.

Shen Nung often went on long journeys to visit his people or to hunt wild animals, and on the way he would refresh himself by drinking freshly-boiled water. Such was the case one day in the year 2737 BC. Whilst the water was still boiling, a few leaves from a nearby tree fell into the water. Soon the liquid had turned a beautiful golden yellow colour and gave off a wonderful smell.

The Emperor tasted the mixture. He found it excellent and felt himself wonderfully refreshed. From that day forth, Shen Nung would drink nothing else and soon his subjects also acquired a taste for the drink. Tea had been invented. Thus far the Chinese legend, whose veracity even orthodox Chinese historians have come to doubt – for in 2737 BC there was neither a unified Chinese Empire nor an Emperor, nor had writing been invented to pass on the story. Furthermore, it is somewhat questionable whether fresh green tea-leaves could have been used to produce such an exquisite drink without any further preparation.

A German explorer, Engelbert Kämpfer (1651–1716), a doctor and the son of a priest from Lemgo in Lippe came across another tea myth from the Far East in the late seventeenth century. Kämpfer had been accompanying expeditions to Russia and Persia for many years. He had also been to Ceylon and India and finally to Indonesia and Japan, where he stayed for two years. His *Amoenitates exoticae*, published in 1712 in his home town and for which he would later be remembered, contains the story of the good Indian Darma, the third son of the Indian King Cosyuvo. Darma was a Buddhist missionary in China. He spent his nights in his religious exercises. One night, after he had accidentally fallen asleep, he angrily ripped out his eye-lids and threw them to the ground. The following morning they had put down roots and sprouted little bushes with evergreen leaves. Darma tasted these leaves and found that by doing so he could shun sleep.

According to Kämpfer, this event occurred in 519 AD. Kämpfer includes in his book a portrait of Darma showing him with enormous eye-lids. Darma was in fact a historical figure who played an important role in bringing Buddhism into China. But the historical Darma died in 495 AD. Legend and historical reality overlap, and it may be assumed that Kämpfer's story contains a grain of truth, even if the part with the eye-lids sounds somewhat improbable.

In another legend there is a further connection between Buddhism and the art of drinking tea. It tells of the Chinese scholar Gan Lu who was converted to Buddhism whilst in India. He returned to China not only with his new faith but also with a small pouch of tea seeds. This must have been long before Darma's miracle, as can be ascertained from a slave contract drawn up in verse form by Wang Pao, the court poet of Emperor Hsün. The contract lays down very precisely which duties a slave has to fulfil. They include the purchase of tea from the market in Wu-Yang, its preparation and serving in cups.

The "Story of the Three Kingdoms" grew up around 270 AD with the story of King Sun Hao and Wei Chao. The King would often invite his friends to convivial banquets and would force his guests to drink at least seven *sheng* (more than a litre) of wine. Wei Chao could never manage more than three *sheng*, no matter how hard he tried. But because he had to pretend that he still liked the wine, he had a friend fill his glass wih tea instead. The King discovered the fraud, sacked Wei Chao from office and had him thrown in jail. Wei Chao was eventually executed in 273 AD.

A few decades earlier the writer Chang Hua (232–300) had discussed the unusual new drink in a far from favourable light. In one chapter entitled "Foods which should be avoided", he warned people against the insomniac qualities of tea. At that particular time, tea was regarded as a medicine to aid digestion or for relaxation, but it was also used in poultices for rheumatism and gout.

The Art of Making Tea in Ancient Times

"Tea is a work of art and requires the hand of a master to draw out its most noble qualities", claimed the Japanese tea sage Kakuzo Okakura in his *Book of Tea*. Okakura said there were three different ways of making tea – boiling tea, "whisking" tea, and brewing tea. The "classical" period during which it was normal practice to boil the tea lasted up until the year 850. The leaves would be steamed, ground up with pestle and mortar, shaped into little cakes with rice, ginger, salt, orange peel, spices, milk and onions, and then boiled. The result was a syrupy mixture of leaves, which would probably have resembled the tea with yak butter which is still served in Tibet today. The Russian custom of serving tea with slices of lemon probably also stems from this origin.

The "romantic" period was the period when tea was "whisked". It lasted throughout the Song dynasty (960–1279). The unfermented (green) leaves would be ground into a fine powder, covered with boiling water and whisked into a thick sauce using a small brush made from bamboo.

The enthusiasm for tea reached new heights during the Song period. Competitions were even held in which new mixtures of tea were tasted and judged. Emperor Hui-tsung (1101–1124) would often pay high prices for rarer teas and even wrote a treatise on twenty different types, in which he prized white tea as the rarest and finest amongst them. Tea-drinking was no longer regarded as a poetic pastime, but was now seen as a path to self-awareness. Wang Yüch'eng claimed that tea "would flood his soul like a beautiful idea and its delicate bitterness was like the aftertaste of sound advice". Su Tung-p'o wrote of its clarity and purity which could vanquish corruption better than a virtuous man. According to Okakura, the monks of Zen in the south would congregate around the statue of Darma "and drank tea from a single bowl as if it were a holy sacrament". The ritual became the foundation for the tea ceremony which was widespread throughout the 15th century and still exists even today.

The third and final "school" of tea, the "naturalistic" school was founded under the

Tea was not only regarded as a drink in China up until 850 AD, it was seen as a food. And it is still regarded as such in present day Tibet, where steamed tea-leaves are ground up with pestle and mortar and then brewed with salt and yak butter to make butter tea.

Ming dynasty (1368–1644). "Whisked" tea was replaced by brewed tea, the process with which we are most familiar with today, and at the same time black tea took the place of green tea.

Lu Yu's Cha Ying

During the era of the T'ang dynasty, from 618 to 907, the period of boiled tea, Lu Yu wrote his *Holy Book of Tea*, the *Cha Ying*, which was to prove a decisive step in the development of the tea culture. Nothing is known about Lu Yu's life, except that he was a poet and philosopher who died in 804 at a very advanced age. His book appeared around 780 AD. According to legend, Lu Yu was abandoned by his parents whilst still very young. A Buddhist priest found him and took him in, seeing in him a disciple. Lu Yu had other ideas. He left his foster father and became a clown in a circus. Later on, already a respected authority on tea, he lived at the court of Emperor Tai-tsung who reigned from 763 to 779. While at court, tea merchants commissioned him to write a book. The *Cha Ying* was a great success and its fame soon spread. But Lu Yu was said to have become a priest and a hermit in later years, thereby fulfilling the wishes of his foster father.

The *Cha Ying* consists of three volumes and ten chapters. In the first, Lu Yu discusses the nature of the tea plant; in the second the instruments for harvesting the tea, and in the third, the selection of the leaves. According to Lu Yu, there are a great many different sorts of leaf which make excellent tea. These include leaves which are "as wrinkled as the leather on the boots of Tartar riders; as frizzy as the hair on a bull's belly; or as smooth as the mist which rises from a mountain gorge; which shimmer like the spray from the sea and are as soft as damp earth".

In the fourth chapter of his book, Lu Yu describes 24 different pieces of equipment used in the preparation of tea – from a ba-

sin standing on three legs to the bamboo cupboard in which all these utensils were kept. In his opinion, cups made from blue glass should be used for drinking tea, because they would emphasise the green colour of the tea, whilst white cups would make it look pink and unappetising.

Lu Yu describes the preparation of tea in the fifth chapter of the *Cha Ying*. With the exception of salt, he rejects all the usual ingredients which were added to tea during the T'ang period. He considered water from a mountain spring best suited for the purpose – river water and ordinary spring water should only be used if there were no alternative. He pinpoints the different degrees of boiling: "When the water first begins to boil, tiny bubbles which look like the eyes of fish appear on the surface of the water and one can hear a soft hissing. Then the water looks like a stream flowing very quickly and one can see a string of pearls at its edge. This is the second degree of boiling. Finally, the water is a mass of wild waves – which is the third degree of boiling." Salt is added during the first degree, tea during the second, and a ladle of cold water is added during the third degree of boiling so that the tea sinks to the bottom and the "water is made young again". The mixture is then poured into bowls and drunk. The experience of drinking tea was described thus by the poet Lo-tung, a contemporary of Lu Yu: "The first cup moistens my lips and throat. The second drives away my loneliness, and the third penetrates my barren soul to uncover some five thousand volumes of ideograms. The fourth cup produces a light sweat – everything bad is disappearing through my pores, and by the fifth, I am purified. The sixth cup has brought me into the realm of the immortal, and the seventh – ah, I cannot drink any further. I can only feel the cool breeze in my sleeves. Where lies *horaisan* (the Chinese heaven)? Let me sail on this breeze until I reach there!"

In the remaining chapters of his book, Lu Yu discusses the everyday methods of tea-drinking and famous tea-drinkers; he describes

The Cha Ying was the first classic in the literature of tea and was written in 780 AD by the
philosopher and poet Lu Yu. Above: An edition dating from 1265 and containing additional articles from periods after Lu Yu's
death.
Right: This tea plant in the south-western province of Yunnan is said to be over 1700 years
old.

variations in the tea ceremony and adds illustrations of the various pieces of equipment used. The tenth and final chapter of the *Cha Ying* has been lost.

The book must have aroused enormous interest in China when it was published for there were many imitations. There were tea experts who claimed they could taste the difference between tea prepared by Lu Yu and tea prepared by one of his disciples. There was even a mandarin who became famous for failing to show due appreciation for tea prepared by the great master.

Lu Yu's *Cha Ying* continued to exercise enormous influence throughout China for many hundreds of years and even began to influence the tea ceremony in Japan. Even when it became commonplace to brew tea, it never lost its importance and this can be seen in a poem of Emperor Kien-long (1711–1799): "Place a three-legged basin over a medium fire, a basin whose colour and shape indicate it has been well-used. Fill it with the water of melted snow. Let the water reach the first degree of boiling, in which fish becomes white and lobster red. Pour the water into a cup of fine leaves. Let it stand a short while, until the first thick clouds of steam have dispersed and only a thin mist floats above the surface. Then slowly drink this exquisite drink which will give you strength against the five cares which trouble your soul. The sweet calm of such a drink can be felt and tasted but never described."

The cultivation of tea had become widespread in China by Lu Yu's time. Most of the tea plantations were in the upper reaches of the Chang Yang (Yangtze Kiang) in the Anhui and Shiyang provinces. The T'ang dynasty made the tea trade a state monopoly. It was the task of the large landowners to transport the tea harvests to the capital, Ch'ang. They were "paid" in scrip, certificates which could be used when buying goods. These certificates were in fact the forerunners of paper money, invented by the Chinese in the year 1024 and were in use long before the system was introduced in Europe.

From the "Mirror of the Ladies of the Green Houses", a collection of Japanese woodcuts, dating from 1776. Three courtesans during the tea ceremony, called chanoyu.

The Tea Cult in Japan

As in many other areas, the Japanese adopted the tea cult from neighbouring China. Tea imported from China was first mentioned in Japan during the Nara period of 709–784. Buddhist priests were the first to use the new drink, which they took medicinally. The layman only began to drink tea during the Hian period (784–1185). The Imperial Court began to encourage the cultivation of tea, but it would only become commonplace during the Kamkura period (1192 onwards) when a Buddhist priest, Eisai Myoan, brought some new seeds from China. The tea cult or *chado* began during the Ashikaga or Muromachi period (1338–1565) but was only to become widespread during the Tokugawa period (1600–1867).

In the year 729, Emperor Shomu (724–748) called upon one hundred priests to help him read the collection of Buddhist writings called *Hannyakyo*. The following day he served them tea. The first known tea culture goes

Few things are required for the tea ceremony. They include a room of about twenty-seven square feet with a small place for a fire in the centre and utensils such as a ladle, a bamboo brush for whisking the green tea and smooth ceramic bowls. In keeping with traditional Japanese architecture, there are thin sliding partitions to separate the living-room (as in the picture here) or the tearoom from a garden of trees and rocks which is situated in an area of elaborate beauty.

back to Saicho, the founder of the Tendai sect. In 805, Saicho grew some tea which had been brought over from China in Sakamoto, Shikagen, not far from Kyoto. Interest in tea waned during the following years but was reawakened in 1168, when the priest Eisai, founder of the Zen sect in Japan, began to grow tea at various places around Fukuoka in Kyushu. The areas around Uji still used today in the cultivation of tea can be traced back to these seeds brought over by Eisai.

The Buddhist priest, Muso Kokushi, is said to have brought the tea ceremony to Japan. In China, he had been given a rack which looked much like a bookcase, called a *daisu* and which was used for holding the various utensils of the tea ritual. Muso used the *daisu* whilst preparing the tea and began to lay down some rules. They were given their classical form in 1564 by the renowned tea master, Sen no Soeki, better known as Rikyu. He wrote them on the wall of the waiting-room in the first tea-house in Higashiyama near Kyoto:

"When all the guests are assembled in the waiting-room, they must announce themselves by striking the wooden board, the *han*.

Only when one is prepared to be cleansed in the water-bath, is one following the true meaning of the teachings.

The guests enter the guestroom as soon as the host comes and asks them to do so. The utensils for the tea and for the food may not be perfect, and the room may not necessarily be in the highest taste. Those who cannot appreciate the naturalness of the rocks and the trees in the tea-garden would do better to leave straight away.

When the boiling water is sighing like the wind as it blows through the pine trees and a bell rings, the guests enter the tea room for the second time. The state of the water and the fire must always be taken into consideration.

From the earliest times, conversations on worldly topics have been forbidden within the tearoom or the tea-garden.

If the meeting is true to the teachings, no flattery in either word or expression is admitted between host and guest.

A meeting may not last more than two hours (four hours by today's reckoning). But no harm is done if that limit is exceeded when the conversation is about Buddhism or aesthetic issues."

These seven rules make up the great law of the tea ceremony and whosoever wishes to enjoy it should abide by them.

What is the secret of the tea ceremony? In his book, Kakuzu Okakura speaks of "tea-ism" as a cult which reveres what is beautiful amidst the ugliness of everyday life. "It encompasses purity and harmony, the secret of compassion, and the romanticism of social order. By its very nature, it is the adoration of the imperfect, for it is a sensitive attempt to perfect the possible amidst the impossibility which we call life."

It was even more than that. Okakura says: "The development of tea-ism has been greatly enhanced by the isolation of Japan from the rest of the world. Our housing, our traditions, our clothing and cuisine, our porcelain, lacqueur and painting, even our literature have all been influenced by it.

No one who has ever studied Japanese culture can ignore it... In colloquial speech, we talk of 'people who have no tea in them' as people who are unreceptive to the tragicomedy of their own existence. And we dismiss any unruly aesthete who allows himself to be swept along by the flood of his unleashed feelings without any consideration for the tragedy of human life, as someone who has 'too much tea' in them."

The Art of Tea and the Tearoom

The Japanese word for the tea ceremony, *chanoyu*, literally means "hot water for tea". A much more appropriate translation would perhaps be "the art of tea", for according to Irmtraud Schaarschmidt-Richter in her essay

One of the rituals of the tea ceremony is the cleansing at the water-bath in the garden. It is said to purify the mind and wash away the social standing of the guests during the ceremony.

on Okakura's book, it is indeed an art form. She states further: "The *chanoyu* is a communal occasion for drinking tea which takes place within a given framework and follows a precise series of movements. However, these movements are completely functional – they are not forced, artificial or superfluous. In fact, they are used only to prepare and serve the tea in its most perfect form. The hand movements produce a rhythm which make use of the whole body and one could talk in abstractions of a ritual dance."

Theoretically, the ceremony could be performed anywhere, but in practice, it took place in a special tearoom leading on to a special tea-garden. Kakuzo Okakura says of the tearoom: "It is a place for the imagination as a temporary refuge for religious feeling. It is a place for emptiness, inasfar as it is almost totally bare, apart from the minimum aesthetic requirements. It is a place of incomplete symmetry, perfect only in the realm of the imagination."

Jovo, a master of tea, laid down the specific requirements of the tearoom in the 15th century. An area equivalent to the size of four-and-a-half *tatami*-mats is required. Host and guests enter the room through separate doors – the door for the guests is so low that the guests have to bow down to enter. In the centre of the room there is a place for the fire and the teapot hangs above it from a point in the roof. The tea utensils are placed within reach of the mat reserved for the host. There is also a small alcove, called a *tokonoma*, where the only piece of decoration in the room is placed – a scroll, a picture, a piece of sculpture or a vase.

The tea-garden, the area where the guests prepare themselves, symbolises a mountainscape, with small trees and bushes, a winding path of paving-stones, and a water-bath, usually a rock which has been hollowed out, where the guests can wash their hands and mouths. At the entrance to the garden, there is often a small reception room where the guests can assemble for a cup of light tea. A covered seat in the garden is a second point at which the guests can wait and it is here that the host comes to welcome his guests. This takes place in silence and both host and guests make their way to the tearoom after ceremonially washing themselves at the water-bath.

The guests enter the tearoom through the low sliding door. Before they take their places on the floor mats or the *zabuton*-cushions, they must show their appreciation of the object in the *tokonoma* alcove. Then follows the so-called *kaiseki* – a small snack consisting of dishes which have been carefully chosen and arranged. Each one of the guests is presented with his own tray or table on which an assortment of bowls is placed. During the meal, the conversation is light-hearted, often touching on the quality of the porcelain in which the meal is served.

After the meal, the guests retreat once again into the garden where they wait for the host to prepare the actual tea ceremony. The host, or often his wife, cleans and airs the tearoom and places the tea utensils in their prescribed order. He once again summons the guests by ringing a small bell or a gong. They come through the garden, wash their hands and mouths once again at the water-bath, and take their places in the tearoom. The teapot is already in place above the fire. There is a smell of incense in the air. The tea-bowls are warmed with a little hot water. Some of the powdered tea is placed in the bowls using a bamboo spoon and hot water is poured onto it from the pot. The guests are offered pieces of cake from a shallow bowl, and then the tea

master dips a bamboo brush (a *chasen*) into the tea-bowls and whisks the tea into a syrupy broth. He hands the bowl to the first guest who will either drink it and hand it back, or take a sip and pass it on to the next guest. Before handing it on, he wipes the place where he has taken a sip with a tea-towel or a piece of paper on which the cake has been served. Once all the guests have taken their turn, they are offered another piece of cake served with a light tea which an assistant has prepared. The host talks to his guests and often, some of the utensils are passed around and admired, especially if they are valuable, or have an interesting history or inscription.

Finally, the host accompanies his guests back into the garden, where they take their leave of him and return to the main gate. The ceremony may last up to four hours or even longer and it is a time "away from everyday life in which the guest can find relief from everything which weighs upon him" (Okakura). "The strict order can give rise to a beautiful feeling of freedom and harmony if it is obeyed voluntarily, and this makes room and object seem one, so that what we have, we can literally call a complete work of art."

The *chanoyu* has been a favourite subject of Japanese paintings and poetry. A famous example is the poem by the poet Keizan called "Keizan no Bun". It says: "I was asked: have you learnt the rules of tea? I answered: Not yet. But I have heard one thing – the taste is bitter, but its bitterness is sweet. The utensils are simple, but their beauty lies in their simplicity. The room is modest, but quiet, and the garden is small, but well-kept. The conversation is intimate, but polite. The meetings are many, the expenditure small. One can enjoy, but one avoids extravagance. These things are what is important, and whoever says it is not so, let him have nothing to do with me."

Where in our culture, children go to dancing classes, their Japanese counterparts go to tea classes, where they are taught the sequence of the tea ceremony and good behaviour – and if they pass, they receive a diploma.

These ceramic bowls and decorative lotus blossoms were made especially for the tea culture in Japan.

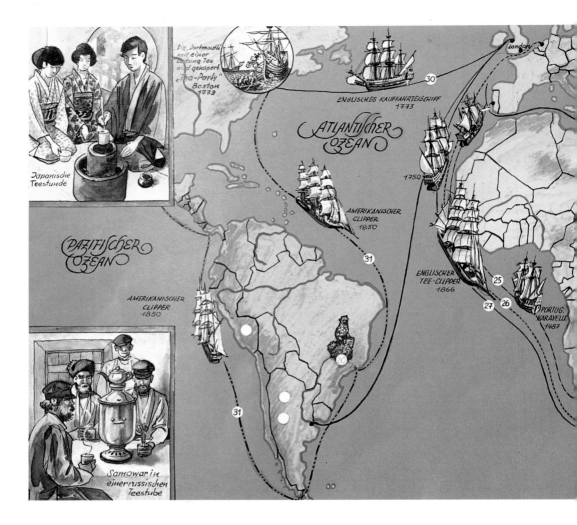

Japanische
Teestunde

ATLANTISCHER
OZEAN

ENGLISCHES KAUFFAHRTEISCHIFF
1773

AMERIKANISCHER
CLIPPER
1850

PAZIFISCHER
OZEAN

AMERIKANISCHER
CLIPPER
1850

ENGLISCHER
TEE-CLIPPER
1866

PORTUG.
KARAVELLE
1487

London

Samowar in
einer russischen
Teestube

Tea in Europe

The Arabs were the first to bring reports of tea to Europe. They had controlled trading from the Far East since the 9th century, both by land and sea. It was they who had brought exotic spices such as pepper, cinnamon, nutmeg and cloves to Europe, as well as incense, silk and green tea. The oldest record of tea deliveries can be traced back to a well-travelled man called Almasudi who lived in the 9th century. The report was not of his own travels, but of a certain Ibn Wahab. Wahab wrote that from the year 879, the Chinese Emperor in Canton received most of his income from the duty on salt and tea. Wahab calls tea *assâch* and it was said that a drink could be made by pouring hot water onto the leaves. The next reports came from 13th-century Persia.

These reports tell how Chinese tea was imported into Persia in small sealed packages. Today, tea historians often wonder that no mention of the plant is made in the writings of Marco Polo (1254–1324) – for he wrote in enormous detail about his twenty-year stay in

Tea was transported mainly by sea. It was a lucrative trade dominated almost exclusively by colonial powers.

the Far East. On one occasion, he mentions a Chinese finance minister who was sacked because he raised the tax on tea. And he also describes the burial traditions in the cemeteries of Japan. It was customary to bury the dead in a sitting position. "A pillow is placed behind the head which points north (the feet always point south), this pillow being filled with tea-leaves." Marco Polo was not impressed. He says: "The Japanese are hardly generous towards their dead – a bit of tea and a box made of soft white wood: no-

thing else. It is hard to believe of a country which is otherwise literally swimming in gold."

Many different theories have been put forward as to why Marco Polo paid so little attention to tea. Was tea so ordinary it was not worth mentioning? Or perhaps it was not drunk at the court of Great Khan – the educated tea experts had left the Imperial court and taken their rituals with them, to south China where the Great Khan had no influence.

*An elaborate label on a tea-chest from Hong Kong. It dates from around 1900
and uses colours fashionable at the time.*

It was not until 1559, through the Italian scholar, Giambattista Ramusio, that Europe received a detailed description of Chinese tea customs and traditions. Ramusio published the travel writings of the Persian merchant, Hadshi Mohammed, who brought both rhubarb and tea to Europe. An ounce of China tea, called *chiai catai*, cost as much as a whole sack of rhubarb.

Arab merchants, Portuguese sailors and Jesuit missionaries were the greatest activists in the spread of tea throughout Europe. In 1633, Alvarez Semedo, a Portuguese Jesuit who travelled extensively throughout China, described the preparation and uses of tea. Pedro Terixeira, also a Portuguese, was drinking green tea exported from China to Molucca at the beginning of the 17th century.

In 1638, Albrecht von Mandelslohe encountered tea-drinking Dutchmen and Englishmen in Surat, north of Bombay, and in 1673, Adam Olearius reported that there were teahouses in Isfahan.

The Netherlands – Europe's First Tea-drinkers

European countries became increasingly interested in trade with the East now that Portugal had established several of its trading centres along coasts of eastern Asia. The Dutch, in particular, sought to profit from Far Eastern delicacies. They founded the Dutch East India Company (V.O.C.) in 1602, which, like the other 17th-century companies, had a trading monopoly and extensive legal powers. Their ships were allowed to carry arms; they were authorised to set up fortress settlements overseas, mint their own coins, raise their own troops and they had their own legal powers. The East India Company took over all the other settlements which had been founded by Dutchmen in eastern India and worked out a plan whereby they could break Portuguese supremacy through founding and extending their other centres. They settled first in Thai-land, then called Siam, and took Ambon. Then they conquered the Portuguese citadel in Tidor and spread to the Moluccas. But it was not only the Portuguese they had to contend with. They also had to do battle with the British who had founded their own East India Company (E.I.C.) in 1600 and had been pursuing a far-sighted colonial policy. It was Dutch ships, however, which brought the first cargo of China tea to Europe in 1610.

The new drink spread fairly rapidly throughout the Netherlands, where it was held in high esteem by physicians and sold by chemists. History's first tea-broker was the businessman Jan Snyder. He found it difficult at first to get rid of his chests of tea. When he met with no success in Amsterdam, he tried to sell them in London. Once again, no one wanted to know and he had to have them brought back to Holland. By this time, he had incurred heavy debts.

Dutch doctors claimed that tea increased physical strength and improved memory; they said it accelerated the workings of the soul and helped thin the blood. They also prescribed it for fever and diarrhoea.

A certain Dr. Dircks, who practised medicine under the pseudonym of Nicolaas Tulp and is immortalised in Rembrandt's famous painting, was also an advocate of the medicinal qualities of tea. In his *Observationes Medicae*, he claimed that tea was a remedy for gallstones and fatigue.

Other consignments of tea soon followed the first one in 1610. On January 2th, 1637, the V.O.C. ordered all her ships to import both Chinese and Japanese tea from India. Trade in green tea was clearly lucrative, even when it did not come by sea, but overland in caravans through Central Asia, the Near East and Russia – a much more expensive route. The tea trade was one of the commercial activities which so enriched 17th-century Holland, as can be seen from the houses of the wealthy merchants of Amsterdam.

Under the well-known sailor, Johannes Maatsuyker, a delegation from the Dutch Company

Paintings of the Chinese and of goods imported from China always had a faintly exotic flavour. These illustrations by two 19th-century English artists depict the processing of tea (above) and the unloading of tea-chests on the Tsin-tang, a tributary of the Zhu Yang (Pearl River) in Canton (right).

Chinoiserie was "flavour of the month" which is probably why Gottfried Bernhard Götz, a well-known fresco painter from Augsburg, produced this painting in 1751. A Chinaman is smoking a hookah (hubble bubble or water-pipe) under a palm tree, whilst being served tea. Götz used the heat in the cup, the stove and the pipe as an allegory for the element of fire. There are similar paintings in the rococo ballroom of Leitheim Castle on the Danube, which contain allegories of the other elements, earth, wind and water.

succeeded in being invited to the Imperial Court in Canton. Maatsuyker received a letter of recommendation from the Manchu Emperor himself, whereby a party of 100 Dutchmen would be allowed to come to China every eight years, only twenty of whom, however, would be allowed to enter the Imperial Court. Thus Canton became the cornerstone of the Chinese tea trade. The Dutchmen would also be supplied with natural silk – both tea and silk would be paid for in silver. A trade overseer in Canton, called the Hoppo, ensured that the courtiers received their fair share of the silver. By the mid-17th century, it was not only the wealthier Dutchmen who were drinking tea – tea was becoming a national drink.

England Turns to Tea

Of the three exotic drinks to establish themselves in 17th-century Europe, coffee, tea and cocoa, the natives of the British Isles at first preferred coffee. In 1650, the first coffee-house on British soil opened in Oxford. It was run by Cirques Jobson, a Syrian Jew, in the eastern part of the town, in the parish of Saint Peter, between Edmund Hall and Queen's College. The chronicler Anthony Wood remarked: "Anyone interested in the new would drink there." Two years later, Pasqua Rosee, a Greek, opened a coffee-house in Cornhill, London. The Middle Eastern merchant Daniel Edwards had brought Rosee back from Ragusa and Rosee would make him Turkish coffee every morning. Edwards' friends then began calling on him every morning to have a cup of Rosee's coffee. Edwards soon tired of this and rented Rosee a room of his own in St. Michael's Alley which soon developed into a lively little coffee-house.

Thomas Garraway called himself a "tobacconist and coffee-man" when he opened his coffee-house at number 3 Change Alley in London in 1657. According to Garraway, tea had also become fit for society by this time, something "quite refined, which could be presented to princes and other great people". Gradually, the customers in the coffee-houses began to show more interest in tea. Every year, the ships of the British East India Company would import ever larger cargoes of tea. In 1690, the figure was no more than 22,000 pounds, but only a hundred years later it had reached 8,8 million pounds. The monopoly East India Company had succeeded in "turning a country of potential coffee-drinkers into a nation of tea-drinkers within a relatively small number of years" (W.H. Ukers in his book *All About Tea* published in 1935). In 1662, Charles II married the Portuguese Princess Catherine of Braganza, who was an ardent tea-drinker and introduced the custom of drinking tea to the English court. This increased the turnover of the tea merchants and was seen as a victory over alcohol, which the lords and ladies had hitherto drunk "morning, noon and night".

Charles did not share his wife's enthusiasm for the new drink. He placed an enormous tax on tea imports and passed a law against the further spread of tea-gardens and coffee-houses which he regarded as the breeding ground for politically undesirable ideas. The tea-drinkers protested to such an extent against this infringement of their new pastime that the king was forced to repeal the law within a few weeks – an event hitherto unique in British history.

However, the tax remained and as a result, tea was a great deal more expensive than on the Continent. Consequently, smuggling also increased and Dutch cutters would come as close as possible to the British coast, where the tea-chests would be loaded onto small boats and brought to land. By the early 19th century, approximately 5,5 million pounds of tea were officially imported into Britain every year. On top of that, a further 7 million pounds were smuggled in. London became the centre of the tea trade. In 1785, there were almost 30,000 tea wholesalers and retailers in the British Isles, as well as almost 2,000 tea houses and coffee-houses.

Tea at every opportunity – it became the great British tradition of the 19th century. The first cup would be drunk every morning in bed, the next at breakfast.

"Low tea" was a light but tasty snack, "Five o'clock tea" came at dusk, and "high tea" was the highlight of the evening in British family life. In the office and at the workplace, it was customary to have several tea-breaks, despite protests that it would prove the downfall of the economy. The protesters were forgetting, however, that a considerable number of firms in England were, and still are closely tied to the tea trade.

Tea as a social drink: around the samovar in the Tsarist Russia (top); at a tea party with gentlemen visitors (above); and in the English manner, in a garden by the Thames at the turn of the century (right).

A cup of tea was appropriate in any situation – in times of worry, or in times of joy, in any difficult situation. A good example of this can be seen in a story from the *News of the World*: "Pauline Jenkins had the shock of her life on her wedding night when she discovered that her newly-wedded husband was a woman. 'I wanted to pack my things and leave straight away,' she told our reporter, 'but instead I went into the kitchen and made myself a cup of tea.'"

The *Süddeutsche Zeitung* had this to say about the story: "In the whole literature of tea, there is no better example of the qualities of a cup of tea – its ability to ease any conflict, to assist in any catastrophe, to soothe any pain, play down any class conflict and to lubricate the complicated machinery of British society." Tea, in England, is an integral part of good society, despite the fact that coffee consumption has considerably increased in recent years, and despite the fact that famous people such as Winston Churchill have stabbed the tea industry in the back by claiming they preferred whisky.

But we must not anticipate our story – let us turn back and look at the effects of tea in other countries.

France, Sweden, Scotland and Russia

The French became aquainted with China tea through the Dutch in 1636. One of tea's earliest fans was Louis XIV. He had learnt that neither the Chinese nor the Japanese suffered from gout or heart attacks because they drank tea. So he drank tea regularly as a medicine against his own gout. Whatever pleased the king would also please his court, and it was the gentlemen in particular who developed a taste for the exotic drink. They surrounded it with a certain amount of Chinese ritual, using the finest porcelain, Chinese carpets and scenery. The ladies preferred cocoa and coffee. Louis' sister-in-law, Liselotte of Pfalz

(1652–1722), also became aquainted with tea at the court of Versailles, but described it as unpalatable: "Tea tastes to me like hay or cow dung! Mon Dieu! How can people like something which tastes so bitter and smells so abominably?", she wrote in one of her famous letters.

Undeterred, the French tried to cultivate the herb in France. In 1658, Dionysus Jonquet planted a few shrubs in the *Jardin des Plantes*, the royal park in Paris – but with little success. The plants flourished in the hothouses but not outdoors. The Parisian climate was not suitable.

The Swedish botanist and natural scientist, Carl Ritter von Linn (Linnaeus) also attempted to cultivate tea, which he called *Camellia thea* because of its similarity to the camellia plant. He tried to acquire some seeds from China but was unsuccessful for many years because the Chinese would not allow any seeds to be taken out of the country.

Furthermore, it could take up to two years to transport tea by sea and the chances of seeds sprouting after that would be severely reduced. A Swedish preacher called Osbek was able to acquire a tea plant in China, which he intended to present to Linnaeus. A storm at the Cape of Good Hope soon destroyed his plan.

Some time later, the commercial attaché, Langerström, presented the botanical gardens in Uppsala where Linnaeus worked, with two shrubs which he took to be tea. After examining the flowers of the plants, it was discovered that they were, in fact, merely camellias – Langerström had been taken for a ride. Another attempt was made with a real tea shrub which had made the journey to a Swedish port. The ship's crew placed the plant on a table in the boat, expecting to return and pick it up later, but while they were gone, rats nibbled at the plant and destroyed it. It was not until October 3rd, 1763 that Captain C.G. Eckeberg was able to present the first well-preserved tea shrub to Linnaeus. It was planted in the botanical gardens where it flourished – but here too, it remained a hothouse plant.

The first attempt to establish tea in **Scotland** met with failure. In 1685, the widow of the Duke of Monmouth sent a packet of tea to some relatives in Scotland. Because there were no instructions on the packet, the leaves were boiled in water and served up as vegetables whilst the water was thrown away!

In the meantime, tea was having great difficulty in becoming established in **France**. On the one hand, it had to compete with the herbal teas which were drunk everywhere in the rural areas, whilst on the other, the French preferred the taste of coffee. Furthermore, doctors claimed that drinking tea was unhealthy. When Jean de Mauvillain published a thesis under the title "Does China Tea Stimulate the Intellect?" in the mid-17th century, he almost caused a riot. A number of doctors openly burnt the work, while others denounced de Mauvillain's supervisor, Dr. Morissot.

Despite these events, many prominent people heartily advocated tea. One of them was Cardinal Mazarin who suffered from a very painful case of gout, another was Madame de Sévigné. The Landgrave of Hesse-Kassel, according to his wife the Princess of Tarent, drank anything up to forty cups a day whereby "his spirits were considerably heightened when he had been so near to death".

The history of tea followed a different course in Tsarist **Russia**. Ivan Petrov and Bornash Yalichev, two Cossacks, were already aware of the existence of the drink from China in 1567. But it was not until 1638 that any considerable amounts of the drink would reach Moscow. The Russian diplomat, Vassily Starkov or Storkov, led a delegation in the same year to the court of the Mongolian Khan. The Khan presented his guests with a few chests of tea as a gift for Tsar Michael I (1596–1645). The Russians were not eager to carry something which they regarded as useless, yet the tea was nevertheless greeted with much excitement at the Imperial court, and soon won many supporters throughout Russia. Tea usually fared better on the long journey over land from China to Europe than in the damp and musty ships, and for centuries, tea brought over by caravan was prized more highly than tea which had been shipped over. Great quantities of tea were sold to European countries via Russia, and in Russia itself, tea became an everyday drink. In the most fashionable households, tea was taken morning and evening, both at home and abroad.

An essential tool in making tea in both Persia and Russia was the *samovar*, the urn. The water was kept hot, often for the whole day, by placing the highly-decorated urn over hot coals. A tiny pot contained the tea extract and whenever someone felt like a cup of tea, they would put some of the extract in a cup and add hot water from the samovar. In Russia, tea is usually drunk with lump sugar with a slice of lemon and sometimes a small sweetmeat or preserves. Russian menus often contain vodka flavoured with tea.

The widest selection of caravan teas could be found in the numerous tea-shops around St. Petersburg. These tea-shops were "the most beautiful in the world – decorated in a European style, combining the luxury of St. Petersburg with the splendour of China, where the arrangement of the teas was most pleasing and the most noble clients came to select and buy their tea". There were over hundred different types. "The sweetest of smells fills the rooms, so that one dearly wishes to remain in these shops forever. The smell of tea is most agreeable to the senses and fills the soul with happiness and light. Only a Dutchman with his nose for edam cheese and pickled herrings would not be enchanted by its perfume" (Baron Eugene von Vaerst, *Gastrosophy* vol. 2).

The times when caravans of tea used to travel the whole breadth of Russia are long gone. "Russian tea" is no longer the name given to tea transported by caravan, it is simply a mixture with a Russian flavour.

There is, however, a plant called "Russian tea" which is grown within the Soviet Union and which can be found elsewhere as well. The first attempts to cultivate tea along the

Crimean coast during the 1840s met with little success. Industrial cultivation did not begin until the 1890s in Georgia on the Black Sea, in areas around Krasnodar and in the Ukraine. Most of the tea today comes from Georgia.

"Russian Tea" has a magic of its own. Not only because the tea is prepared in a samovar, but because of the ingredients added to it – cinnamon, a slice of lemon, candied fruits and sometimes even a glass of vodka. Earlier, Russian tea was the name given to the costly teas which had been brought to Europe overland by caravan.

Let yourself be transported into a world of perfumes and delicious tastes. In this pretty little tea-shop in Bremen you can find hundreds of different types of tea, including herbal teas. You can also choose from a wide range of ingredients for an extensive breakfast or a leisurely tea-time.

Germany's Tea Drinkers

Tea is first mentioned in Germany in 1650 in some old price-lists from a number of apothecaries. *Herbea thea* appears in a list in Nordhausen in 1657. It appears again in a list in Liegnitz and in a list in Ulm in 1662. Dr. Cornelius Dekker (1647–1685), a doctor from the Netherlands, is generally considered to be one of the first and most important promoters of tea of the time. He was born in Alkmaar and studied in Leiden under the respected physician, Franciscus Sylvius. He practiced in both Amsterdam and Hamburg, before being called to Berlin by the Great Elector Frederick William to be his personal physician. He was also made a professor at the University of Frankfurt-on-the-Oder. Dekker is perhaps better known under his nickname Bontekoe which is derived from the figure of a cow in his father's house. Dr. Bontekoe fed much of his journalistic energy into promoting the uses of tea. His "Tract on the Most Excellent Herb, Tea", for example, appeared in 1679 and a few years later he published another one entitled "The Uses and Misuses of Tea". He believed that tea could be used to cure all ailments, not just the Elector's gout. "Tea gives new life and new strength to anyone who is at the end of his tether," he claimed, "even to those who already have one foot in the grave". After drinking a sufficient amount of tea, a man would feel "brave, hearty, strong, happy and full of energy" – a sufficient amount of tea being about fifty cups a day! But it could even be more – the limit being about two hundred. According to Bontekoe, tea had nine different restorative effects: "The first is in the mouth, the next in the stomach, the third is in the bowels, the fourth in the blood, the fifth in the brain, the sixth against drunkenness, the seventh against scurvy, the eighth outshines baths and warm water, and the ninth against fever."

But tea could not cure all things – one day, when he was only 38 years old, the doctor himself had a fatal fall down the steps of the palace in Berlin. No medicine could save him. The career of Dr. Bontekoe had come to a premature end, and the rumours which had been circulating, that Bontekoe was being bribed by the Dutch East India Company, could not now come under investigation. Nevertheless, with all his tea propaganda, Bontekoe had played his part in turning people away from more harmful drinks such as schnaps, beer and wine.

The notion of tea as a cure-all can be seen in a poem printed in a pamphlet called the "Complete Natural and Mineral Store" which dates from 1700:

Wouldst thou care for thy health,
Against any shape of disease,
Wouldst thou live long,
Thou shouldst hearken unto me:
Noble tea is the recipe!
For by its virtue,
We shall remain forever young.

The theme of tea, its literature and research is inexhaustible. It almost goes without saying, that poets such as Goethe drank tea instead of wine. Indeed, tea-parties are frequently mentioned in Goethe's work. Eckermann notes in autumn 1823: "Goethe invited me to tea this evening with many other people. I enjoyed myself. The atmosphere was relaxed and unforced. People sat around, laughed and made jokes. Goethe went from one person to another and seemed more content to listen to his guests and let them talk, than say anything himself."

Heinrich Heine was more sceptical about the drink. He tells us of a stay in Norderney in 1826 and says of his hosts: "They had even reached more southern lands in their ships, where the sun shines more brilliantly, and the moon more romantically. Yet all the flowers in the world could not fill the hole in their hearts, and amidst the infinite perfumes of spring's kingdom, they longed to be back on their islands of sand, in their tiny huts, by their flickering fires, where they could sit in their woollen jackets and drink their teas made of sea-water, which vary in name only."

Sitting on the terrace of a café in Berlin called Stehely, Heine wrote some of his most famous tea poems, in which he mocks the sentimentalism of 19th-century German bourgeois society, known as Biedermeier:

Sie saßen und tranken am Teetisch
Und sprachen von Liebe viel.
Die Herren, die waren ästhetisch,
Die Damen von zartem Gefühl.

(You sit and drink at the tea-table
And talk about love a great deal.
The gentlemen claim to be aesthetes
The ladies, how sensitive they feel.)

Karl August Varnhagen, whose wife Rahel Varnhagen, was a leading figure in contemporary society and had a literary salon, also mentions the aesthetic teas of the Biedermeier period in his *Memorabilia*: "The light blue rooms were spacious, overlooking the street and tall trees in the garden behind. It was all very simple, there were no luxuries. A few paintings hung on the walls, two busts of Prince Louis Ferdinand and Schleiermacher were situated between some jardinières and only the most utilitarian items of silverware were displayed. Nevertheless, the whole impression was one of elegance. Furthermore, it was all so comfortable and pleasant that one felt that contentment which only the most elegant surroundings are supposed to make one feel, but which, with all the will in the world, is often found wanting."

Rainer Maria Rilke was a tea-drinker ("She sat like the others at tea. It seemed to me at first, as if she were holding her cup slightly differently. One time she smiled. It almost hurt." These lines are from his poem "Die Erblindende"); so too was Ludwig Uhland

("In India's mythical forests, where spring is ever renewed, tea, a myth of its own, forever blossoms and grows").

It was thanks to tea that Heinrich Schliemann had enough money to excavate the city of Troy – part of his wealth came from the tea trade. As he explains in his memoirs: "When cotton became too expensive, I did business in tea, which we had been allowed to ship from May 1862. My first order to Messrs. J. Henry Schröder & Co. in London was for thirty chests. When these had been sold profitably, I ordered 1,000, then 4,000 and 6,000 more. I then bought a whole warehouse from Messr. J. E. Günzburg in St. Petersburg for a very reasonable price because he wanted to retire. In the first six months, I earned 140,000 marks from tea."

Annette von Droste-Hülshoff also paid tribute to Chinese tea in a poem entitled "The Teatable". In the poem, she describes a party at which, "The drink of the pigtailed Chinese hisses in a silver kettle". The ladies are busy with their knitting, whilst the gentlemen display "the jewels of their wisdom". It is a very Chinese affair and in the last verse, we read:

Quietly now, take your hat and coat,
Go quickly, while they are reading!
Or, I swear by my mother's blood,
That they'll turn you into a Chinaman.

Let us return to Goethe. In 1806, he finally married his longtime companion, Christiane Vulpius. Weimar society was reluctant to accept her as Frau Goethe and at one tea party, they discussed whether or not she should be accorded an invitation. Louise von Göchhausen, a lady of the court, said: "If Goethe has given her his name, I think we could give her a cup of tea."

The Frisians and Tea

Of the various tea-drinking regions in Germany, Friesland, and East Friesland in particular, are of special significance. For many years, the Frisians have been the most enthusiastic consumers of tea – Friesland receives a quarter of all tea imports in the Federal Republic, although only four per cent of the German population actually lives there. One reason for this excessive love of tea is the fact that Friesland is situated next to the Netherlands. During the 17th century, the Netherlands supplied tea to the whole of Germany and especially neighbouring East Friesland, which had temporarily been a part of the Netherlands. The exact time when East Friesland first became acquainted with tea is uncertain, but there is one report of a ship from Hamburg which ran aground on a sand bank between Baltrum and Langeoog in 1694. The fishermen from Westeraccumersiel recovered some of the cargo which included a chest of tea. It is said that the inhabitants took the tea to be dried vegetables and made a hearty soup out of it with some lard! Only later on did they learn how to prepare an aromatic drink from the leaves.

A trading company called the "Royal Prussian Asiatic Company in Emden for Canton and China" was founded in Prussia in 1751. The company was based on the same principles as the Dutch and British trading companies. Merchants from Emden, Westphalia, France and the Netherlands, as well as the Prussian state were all involved in the enterprise. King Frederick II – Frederick the Great – even went to Emden himself to sign the papers. His main concern was reduce the amount of money paid to the British and Dutch firms – it would be cheaper for Germany to build up its own trade. On July 6 1753, Emden saw its first consignment of tea arrive on a ship called "King of Prussia". But the king then went a step further. In 1755, he announced that "henceforward, no teas other than those of the Asiatic Trading Company in Emden shall be allowed to enter our royal lands".

It was too good to last. After the temporary occupation of East Friesland in 1757 by the French during the Seven Years War, the company closed its doors in 1765. From now on, East Frisian ships would have to supply the tea themselves, with the support of a whole fleet of Dutch ships registered in the East Frisian ports. They also supplied tea to the West coast of Schleswig-Holstein, the provinces of Dithmarschen and Heligoland.

In 1768, Frederick the Great started a "tea war". He instructed his authorities to restrict the consumption of tea and coffee, with a view to eventually stopping it altogether. The East Frisians would have to be content with beer and other drinks. But they would have none of it – as can be seen in a declaration made in their regional parliament in 1779: "The consumption of tea and coffee is so widespread and so deeply engrained in these parts, that our people would have to change their very beings if they were to bid these drinks farewell!"

Frederick lost the war on tea – Napoleon came next with his Continental Blockade which cut off most of the country's imports. As a result, a very lively black market developed. British ships stored their cargoes on the island of Heligoland, where the East Frisians could collect what they needed. Tea, coffee and sugar loaves became more expensive. A pound of tea cost the equivalent of 15 1/2 pounds of butter, a pound of loaf sugar, the equivalent of 22 pounds of rye bread. The French, who now ruled the country, put the Heligoland smugglers to death. Matters only improved when the German Wars of Liberation released these provinces from the French rule.

Taxes and customs duties continued to weigh heavily on the tea trade and later on came the rationing of the two World Wars. In 1939, the new tea-ration cards allowed a monthly ration of only twenty grams (less than one ounce) per person. That had been the normal daily consumption hitherto. The ration was eventually raised to thirty grams (just over one ounce) a month, but that was hardly much of an improvement. Seasoned tea-drinkers would complain: "We will die if we have no tea." Occasionally, people were given a little extra – and there was a lively black market. Rationing ended in 1949, but it was replaced by an extremely high tax on tea.

The black market continued. Smugglers who hid the tea in the false bottoms of their cars, or women who sewed it into the lining of their skirts were imprisoned or heavily fined.

Those times are long gone. Anyone can now afford an East Frisian blend of tea – a blend of highly-flavoured Assam or milder Java tea. The East Frisians drink their tea very strong, poured over a lump of sugar (*kluntje*) and covered with a thick layer of cream (*wulkje room*). A minimum of three cups are drunk, for "three is the customary figure". The favourite times are eleven o'clock in the morning (*elfuehrtje*) or three o'clock in the afternoon (*teetied*), but it is also drunk at other times – after rising in the morning, or before going to bed at night. There is always time for a *lekker Koppke Tee* (a tasty cup of tea) – although you must not think the East Frisians spend their whole day drinking tea. Should you ever be invited to an East Frisian tea party, you will see that the guests will be offered tea until they place their spoon in their empty cup. In olden times, it was customary to place the empty cup upside down on the saucer. Never boast about the tea you drink at home – an East Frisian regards it as no more than *Spölwater* (dishwater).

If tea had to be smuggled into Friesland today, this particular boat would probably be the one to use.

The USA – the Nation Born of Tea

It was the Dutch who brought the first tea to the North American colonies. In 1626, Peter Minnewit (around 1580–1641), a German coloniser working for the Dutch, founded the trading centre of New Amsterdam on the barren granite island of Manhattan which he had bought from the Indians. British colonists conquered the settlement, which then had 1,500 inhabitants, in 1664. They changed its name to New York and made it the capital of the colonies. It is said that the Dutch settlers did not really know what to do with tea. They made a brown, syrupy broth from the leaves and then mixed the leaves with a little salt and butter and ate them as a vegetable.

After the British had settled in New York, the Dutch tea-ships had no further business there. Tea-clippers from the British East India Company took their place and supplied the settlers with their beloved tea. The journey from China via London to New York brought financial rewards, because a high duty on tea had to be paid in London before it was shipped across to America. Further duties then had to be paid to the British authorities when it landed in New York. The mother country was therefore being paid double for every ounce of tea. This did not please the inhabitants of New England. Increasingly, they turned to the cheaper tea smuggled in from the Dutch East India Company. In 1766, British ships imported six million pounds of tea into New York. Dutch ships imported four and a half million. In addition, large amounts of tea were smuggled in.

In 1770, all taxes on British goods imported into the American colonies were abolished – with the exception of the tea tax. Tea was now being imported direct from China to New York, but the duties still had to be paid. From 1765, secret societies sprang up which called themselves the "Sons of Liberty". They fought against the taxation policy of the British and managed to stop all exports of tobacco to England. They also boycotted all tea shipments by the British East India Company, managed to dissuade the tax collectors from doing their job and persuaded businessmen not to buy British goods. The boycott was lifted only a few years later in 1773. Boston, as the centre of the tea trade, was the only city to disagree and that led to an event which was to prove decisive.

During the first few months of 1773, the British East India Company found itself in a critical situation. They had bought in huge supplies of tea which they could not sell in London. Their only chance was to ship it to America. The government in London agreed and allowed it to be imported duty-free into the new colonies – only the basic duty of threepence would still stand. In this way, the company was in a position to supply tea cheaper than the independent traders and the smugglers. So 500,000 pounds were loaded onto three ships, the "Dartmouth", the "Beaver" and the "Eleanor", and they began their journey to the colonies.

However, this arrangement did not please the New Americans. Their anger was directed less at the minimal amount of duty than at the monopoly held by the East India Company. As the tea-ships entered Boston harbour, there were mass demonstrations calling for the tea to be returned to England without any payments of tax. The British Governor, however, a man called Hutchinson, would not allow this.

As the tea-ships would only be allowed to leave the port of Boston again after paying tax on the tea, a party of the "Sons of Liberty" stole on board the three ships disguised as Mohicans and threw 342 chests into the sea. Similar protests occurred in other ports along the East coast. It eventually led to open rebellion. At the battle of Lexington, the freedom fighters under George Washington and a Prussian General Steuben won the decisive

The Boston Tea Party 1773 – the trigger for the fight for independence of the future United States of America. The freedom fighters disguised themselves as Indians when they threw chests full of tea over board as a protest against the import duties of the British government.

victory over the English. Thus the Boston Tea Party signified the birth of the USA. A memorial placard in the port of Boston reads: "Here was once Griffin's Quai where on 16th December, 1773, three British ships and their cargoes of tea lay anchored. Around ninety citizens of Boston, some in Indian costume, stole on board ship to protest against King George's trivial but tyrannical tax of three-pence for every pound, and threw the cargo consisting of 342 chests into the sea. The patriotism of this act, known as the Boston Tea Party, resounded throughout the world." Although the Americans no longer paid any taxes on tea, they were never able to re-establish a balanced relationship with the drink, in contrast to the British who drank increasing amounts of it and obediently paid their taxes.

The United States of America became the largest consumer of coffee in the world, a position it still holds today.

The Tea-clipper Regattas

Time and time again we read of the economic competition between the United States and Europe. And although the spirit of that competition manifested itself primarily in sport throughout the 19th century, it must be remembered that many hard battles were fought for markets and profits. In any case, several of the most important technological revolutions in transport can be traced back to tea.

The fast and sturdy tea ships of the mid-19th century were called "clippers", and it was they who brought the freshly-harvested teas from China to Europe and America.

The British East India Company, founded in 1600 to handle the spice trade, made most of its later money from tea. The Company's stolid and clumsy ships, known as "Indiamen" had been in no hurry because they held the monopoly. All this changed when the monopoly was lifted in 1834. There were now other competitors, and because fresh tea fetched a higher price, the tea-ships were in a greater hurry to reach London and New York from Canton and Hong Kong. The older ships could not travel at such speeds. Only the North American Baltimore Clippers were fast enough, and they were too small to carry tea. So, in 1845, a larger class of clipper was launched in New York. It was called the "Rainbow", and could carry a cargo of 750 tonnes. It was able to recover building costs on her maiden voyage to China and back. In contrast to the normal sailing ships which could only reach a speed of about six knots, the new tea-clippers could travel at about 16, 18 or even 20 knots. "Sovereign of the Seas" and "Flying Cloud" were two of the fastest sailing ships of all time.

Three men were mainly responsible for the record-breaking speeds of the American clippers. The first of these was John Willis Smith, the first ship-builder to establish the new line. Smith, the son of a ship-builder, was not satisfied with rough calculations when it came to ship construction. He studied mathematics and physics and installed his own water-tank to test out his prototypes. He invented a new type of vessel with a sleek hull, sharp bows and a very tall mast. Next came Robert W. Waterman. This sea-captain had been very successful as the master of clippers and he used his experience in the construction of the new ships. Between them, Smith and Waterman built the "Sea Witch", which Waterman captained on a voyage from Hong Kong to New York which took only 74 days and 14 hours – a record which would never be broken. The third member of the team was

neither constructor, nor sailor. His name was Matthew Fontaine Maury and he was a statistician. He studied thousands of old log-books and drew up complex and detailed charts and tables of weather and sea conditions, which captains and navigators could use to help them choose the quickest and best routes. Maury's wind and current charts did away with many traditional preconceptions. More than a thousand sea-captains made use of Maury's up-to-date statistics. By 1854, the statistician had processed over one million separate pieces of data – 380,284 items about the Atlantic Ocean Gulf Stream alone. "Before I laid hands on your work," wrote Captain Phinney of the clipper "Gertrude" to the "pathfinder of the sea", "I crossed the oceans with my eyes closed".

As the speed of the American tea-clippers increased, so did the agitation among British ship owners. Soon they were building their own clippers and the ship-builders along the Thames were channelling all their sporting ambitions into building faster ships than the Americans. "We must take up the challenge of our vast, unleashed opponent", wrote *The Times*. "We must simply use our long-standing experience, our tireless industry and sheer stubbornness to win in the face of their youthfulness, inventiveness and enthusiasm. It is a race of the father against his own son. We are driven by merciless necessity and we must not lose. Let our businessmen and ship-builders heed this warning."

The warning was heeded. The British clippers may have been smaller than the Yankee clippers, but they were just as fast. Before long, ship-building had reached a frenzied pace in both Britain and America. In the fifteen years of the Golden Age of the Clipper, well over five hundred ships were built and one speed record after another was broken.

Perhaps the most famous of the clipper races was the "Great Tea Race" of 1866. Sixteen ships took up the challenge. They lay anchored under the pagodas of the river port of Foo-Chow. Only five had any real chance of winning. These were the "Serica", under Captain George Innes, the "Taeping" under Donald McKinnon, the "Fiery Cross" commanded by Richard Robinson, the "Taitsing" under Daniel Nutsford and the "Ariel", commanded by Captain John Keay.

Cargo-loading began on May 24th; five days later, the "Ariel" had 1,108,000 pounds of tea on board and was ready to sail. She weighed anchor three hours after the last tea-chest had been put into place and was led up the winding Min river to the open sea by a tugboat, the "Island Queen". The tug was not strong enough, however, and the pilot-ship capsized. It had only reached the estuary when the "Fiery Cross" overtook it, and both the "Taeping" and the "Serica" caught up. the "Taitsing" followed close behind. The total distance to be covered was 13,200 nautical miles. The five ships reached the Sunda Strait, crossed the Indian Ocean in full sail, passed Mauritius and headed for the Cape of Good Hope. On August 4th, the "Ariel", the "Fiery Cross" and the "Taeping" crossed the equator – the other two ships were no longer in the running. The leaders continued up the coast of Africa, past the Azores, the Bay of Biscay and into the English Channel. At 1.30 am, Captain Keay of the "Ariel" sighted the Bishop and St. Agnes light off the south coast of England. He set full sail and headed along the English Channel, but by evening, he sighted one of his rivals, the "Taeping", off his starboard bow. By September 5th, both the "Ariel" and the "Taeping" were involved in a wild chase along the Channel. At Dungeness, both clippers took pilots on board. By the time they had reached the Downs, the "Ariel" was still one nautical mile ahead of the "Taeping". At a speed of 14 knots, that was only eight minutes difference – a nominal amount after sailing 13,200 nautical miles in 99 days. There was still no outright winner. By 9.00 pm, the "Ariel" had reached the East India Dock but could not berth because of the low tide. In the meantime, the "Taeping" had sailed past her into the London Dock, where she berthed at 10.00 pm – she had a smaller draught. On September 7th, the "Taeping" was declared the winner. The prize and bonus were divided between the two ships, however, which did not please the public. For weeks afterwards, newspapers discussed whether the "Ariel" should have been declared the outright winner.

The "Serica" docked on the evening of September 6, and the "Fiery Cross" and the "Taitsing" followed two days later.

But the age of the clipper was coming to an end. The Suez Canal was opened in 1869, but it was not suitable for sailing ships. Steamships were now being built and would eventually come to dominate the high seas, but it would be a long time yet before they could overtake the clippers. The elegance of the tall ships can still be admired today in 19th-century pictures and models. The "Cutty Sark", probably the most famous clipper of them all, can still be visited at Greenwich, near London. The "Cutty Sark" was the jewel in the crown of the age of sailing. The name, which means "short shirt", can be traced back to a Scottish legend. There was once a peasant called Tam O'Shanter. One stormy night, he was riding home across a graveyard. In the glow of the lightning, he spied a coven of witches dancing in a circle. One of them was young and pretty and she was wearing a provocatively short shirt (cutty sark in Scots dialect). It was the name a Scotsman called Jock Willis gave to the tea-clipper he commissioned in 1868. For ten years, the "Cutty Sark" worked the tea routes. Later, she transported sheep's wool from Australia, and spent the last years of her working life as a hard coal freighter for the more modern steamships.

The tea trade was the driving force behind the development of technology. This clipper, the "Flying Cloud", symbolises the heyday of the sailing ship. From 1850 onwards, ever larger and faster ships were being built in Britain and America. One speed record after another was broken. This meant that tea could be delivered fresh to trading centres many thousands of miles distant. Then the Suez Canal was opened, and it could only be used by steamships. The fast clippers were no longer in demand, for even with their higher speeds, the route they had to take around the southernmost tip of Africa was infinitely longer.

Tea Cultivation Around the World

There is not a single country in the world which has not tried to grow tea, now that India and Sri Lanka (Ceylon) have come to dominate the world market. It must be said, however, that most countries have not had much success.

Tea cultivation in **India**, probably the most extensive in the world, can be traced back to the efforts of the British colonialists. However, tea-growing in the sub-continent cannot be lumped together under the general term, "Indian tea". There are separate tea-growing areas in the north and the south of the country which produce very distinctive types of tea.

The first attempts to cultivate tea in India date back to the 18th century. Around 1780, a British colonel named Kyd planted a few tea shrubs from Canton in Calcutta. The results were promising and they convinced Sir Joseph Banks, who had accompanied Captain Cook on his voyage around the world, to try and persuade the British East India Company to cultivate their own tea. As the company earned a great deal of money from the tea trade with China and did not want to compete with itself, his arguments fell on deaf ears.

Assam. In 1823, a British major, Robert Bruce, discovered wild tea shrubs growing on the slopes of the Manipur Mountains of Assam and Burma. Dr. Wallich, a scientist from the botanical gardens in Calcutta, was not sure at first whether the plant really was tea, but a second report from one Andrew Charlton, an officer in the Assam Light Infantry, soon convinced him and other scientists. The plants found by Charlton in Upper Assam and by the botanists McClelland and Griffith near Sadiya in Lakhimpur were, in actual fact, a type of tea, and it was assumed at first that they must be related in some way to China tea, *Thea sinensis*. The plants were given the name *Thea assamica*. People still did not believe that they were genuine tea plants, but thought they were some derivative. China tea shrubs were therefore brought over to Calcutta and planted in areas such as Assam. Only later would the native Assam variety be cultivated, and later still China and Assam teas were crossed to produce the hybrids grown on most plantations today.

A company in London, the Assam Tea Company, took over tea cultivation in Assam province in 1839. It was a powerful company with a lot of capital and it succeeded in growing tea on both sides of the Brahmaputra River, despite many obstacles and even though some claimed that growing tea in Assam was tantamount to throwing money into the Brahmaputra.

Darjeeling. Another tea-growing area was discovered on the slopes of the Himalayas in the Darjeeling region. We have the Governor-General of Calcutta, Lord William Bentick, to thank for that. Lord William founded a committee which aimed to break the Chinese monopoly on tea. In 1838, only four years after the founding of the committee, a ship with the first consignment of twelve chests of Assam tea set sail from Calcutta. Many other tea-growing regions were discovered in the years that followed. Today, tea comes from Assam, Dooars and Darjeeling in northern India, and from Nilgiri and Travancore in the south. In the Assam region alone there are over two thousand tea plantations. They produce a strong, aromatic tea which serves as a good basis for blending. Darjeeling, on the other hand, is characterised by a sweet, subtle aroma and is probably the most popular tea.

Once tea cultivation began in India, the British East India Company was no longer able to control trade. The company's monopoly ran out in 1835 and was not renewed.

The situation was very different on the island of **Ceylon**, which is now called Sri Lanka. Between 1656 and 1796, Ceylon was occupied by the Dutch. The English followed and turned the whole island into one vast coffee

The younger and more tender the leaves and buds from the tea plant are when they are picked, the subtler the aroma is in the final drink.

plantation. Quinine and Ceylon cinnamon were also produced. During the second half of the 19th century however, coffee cultivation began to decline. Plant pests and diseases began to infest the plantations and destroyed the coffee plants. It was high time to look for another means of income. A young Scotsman named James Taylor, made the first move. He obtained some tea shrubs from China and Assam and planted them on a small plantation in Loolecondera – with great success. A tea merchant called Thomas Lipton from London bought up a whole row of former coffee plantations which were going cheap, changed them over to tea and supervised the complete process, from production to marketing.

Within a few years, Ceylon had become one of the world's leading suppliers of tea. The main regions are Uva in the east, Dimbula and Dic-koya in the west, and the highlands of Nuwara Eliya in between. The plantation workers in the highlands are Tamils who were brought over from southern India. After being without a state of their own for a long time, some of these Tamils were given citizenship of the island. More were sent back to India. The conflict between the native Tamil and Singhalese populations in Sri Lanka still remains unresolved.

Indonesia. Tea was first brought to Java in 1826. Dr. Philipp Franz von Siebold, a naturalist, was asked by the Agricultural Commission in Batavia (now known as Djakarta) to send several hundred Japanese tea plants to Java, which were then planted and cultivated in the East Indies botanical gardens at Buitenzorg. A tea merchant from Rotterdam called Jacobsen, who had worked

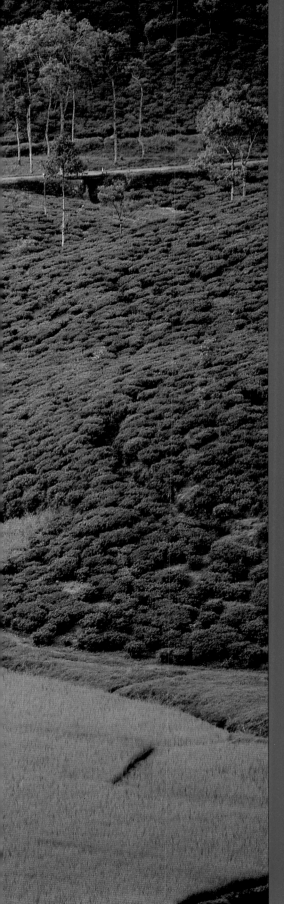

The work involved in the cultivation and production of tea is arduous. Left: An impression of the famous Nuwara Eliya region in Ceylon/ Sri Lanka. Above: A tea picker on the same island. She picks up to 66 pounds of fresh tea-leaves a day, some tens of thousands of shoots.

Dawn on the plantation of Rancabolang, West Java, south of Bandung. Volcanoes dominate the landscape; the climate enables tea to grow all year round.

in all aspects of the tea industry in China for many years, then decided he could use his experience in Java. In 1829, he presented the government of the Dutch East Indies with the first chests of green and black tea. In the same year, Jacobsen brought back some tea shrubs from China. They were planted in Chiserup and their seeds were used to start a large number of plantations. By 1833, there were 500,000 tea plants in the Krawang province alone. Prior to 1865, tea cultivation was supervised on Java by the Dutch colonial government, who then left tea-growing to private businessmen. From 1873, Assam hybrid tea plants began to replace the old Chinese plants.

It was not until the 20th century that Sumatra began cultivating tea. Large plantations sprang up on the east coast, using the most modern agricultural techniques. In most countries, Indonesian tea is used mainly as a base for blends, but Indonesia also produces high quality teas, comparable to those from Assam and Ceylon. Indonesian tea is mainly imported into the European ports of Antwerp, Amsterdam, Rotterdam, Bremen and Hamburg.

Africa. Kenya is by far the most important of the African tea-growing countries. Both, speciality and the more popular teas are grown in the fertile plantations in the highlands of the Kericho region, where they were originally

planted by the British. Malawi and Mozambique, where the Portuguese established the first plantations, and Tanzania and Cameroon where the Germans planted tea, are other African tea-growing countries. South Africa also produces tea but in much smaller quantities.

The first attempts to grow tea in **Brazil**, in 1810, met with no lasting success. This was because Brazilians prefer coffee and yerba-maté tea, which are much easier to grow.

Guatemala, on the other hand, has been very successful at tea-growing. Whether tea will continue to grow there, remains to be seen.

Attempts to cultivate tea in the **United States**, especially in California, South Carolina and Texas, were abandoned because the climate was unsuitable.

In **Australia**, only Queensland has the right climate for growing tea.

What little tea is grown in **Turkey** and **Iran** is used solely for domestic requirements. The same is true of the Soviet Republic of Georgia where extra tea must be imported.

Taiwan, like China, produces mainly green tea and partly- fermented Oolong. Mauritius, Jamaica, the Azores, Fiji and Borneo also attempted to grow tea before World War II, but only **Mauritius** has had any significant success. **Vietnam** has been able to build up its production (consisting exclusively of green tea) once again after the long years of war.

Tea – the Cultivated Plant

There are two different types of tea plant, *Thea (Camellia) sinensis*, Chinese tea, and *Thea (Camellia) assamica*, Assam tea. It is still not known which was the original tea plant. The name *Thea* was current as early as the 17th century, but it was first used as a botanical name by Linnaeus and Engelbert Kämpfer. The name by which tea is known throughout most of China is *cha* or *chia*, a word which has found its way into Japanese *tsya*, Russian *tchai* and Portuguese *chà*. The other European words for the plant *tea, té, thé, Tee* and the Latin *Thea* derive from the names used in southern China – *tia, tai* or *ta*. The stems of the Chinese tea plant can grow to a height of thirteen feet, whilst those of the Assam tea plant can reach heights of over 65 feet if left unattended. Both types are evergreen and have taproots which can grow to a length of 15 feet. The leaves of both plants have short stalks and a leathery surface. They are lanceolate, elliptical and uniform, and have a serrated edge. The leafbuds and young leaves have tiny hairs on their undersides and a silky, silvery sheen. The leaves of the Assam tea plant are noticeably larger than those of the China tea plant. The flowers look like jasmine and are arranged singly or in clusters at the base of the leaves. The round berries are divided into three sections, each containing between one and three seeds the size of a cherry stone.

The tea shrub can grow from sea level to heights of up to 7,000 feet and more in tropical regions. China tea is hardier than Assam tea and can survive temperatures as low as minus 3 °C. Both types need humidity and regular rainfall. The soil should be porous, loosely packed and slightly acidic. It is most important that the soil should not retain water and for this reason tea grows best on sunny mountain slopes.

Traditionally, the plants are grown from the seed. The seedlings are grown in a bed and then transferred to the plantation. In recent years, however, cuttings have been used, and scions are often grafted onto the rootstock. The young plants are pruned regularly so that they will continue to grow but remain at a height of around three or four feet in order to facilitate picking by hand. While the shrubs are young and at ground level, they must be weeded regularly. Pests and diseases must be destroyed biologically wherever possible and the fertilizer should contain nitrogen.

New plantations can generally be harvested regularly after three years in the tropics and after five in the subtropics. This is done by hand – machinery is used only for tilling the soil and transporting the crop. The best teas are made from the buds and the top two leaves ("two leaves and a bud", as the saying goes); the lower, older leaves are only used for making cheaper teas. In equatorial regions, leaves are picked every seven or ten days all year round. Only during the rainy season or during periods of slow growth are the pickers granted a rest.

Experienced pickers can pick between 22 and 25 pounds a day in China, and in Assam, they can pick up to 75 pounds. In China, it takes about 3,200 shoots or "flushes" to produce one pound of tea, whereas in Assam, only about one-third as many are needed.

A great deal of skill is required to pick between 10,000 and 30,000 shoots a day. The leaves are collected into a basket and taken direct to the processing plant or to a collection point, where they are weighed and credited to the picker. The process must be very fast so that the leaves will not begin to ferment in the hot sun and spoil the quality of the tea. In "Imperial picking" only the bud and one extra leaf find their way into the basket. Teas of this sort were picked exclusively for the Imperial Court or for the highest mandarins. The pickers, who had to be virgins, were equipped with golden scissors, and they

Hitherto, picking by machine (as shown here with green tea in Japan) has not been very widespread. High quality teas should contain only "two leaves and a bud", and these have to be picked by hand.

carefully laid the buds into baskets made of gold. Since China no longer has an emperor, "imperial picking" is now a part of history. "Fine picking" is when only the bud and two uppermost leaves are picked. This process is quite costly and reserved only for the best quality teas. The most common process is the third category, "coarse picking", but it is not exclusive enough for some tea-lovers.

The season in which the leaves are harvested is also important. The delicate teas of the "first flush" are harvested after the north-eastern monsoons in northern India. The heavier, spicier teas of the "second flush" follow between May and the end of June. The "rain teas" are harvested during the south-western monsoons of August and October and the "autumnals" or "autumn teas", during the cooler winter months. Despite claims to the contrary, the quality of these later teas cannot compare with the teas of the "second flush". There are no harvests between November and March in northern India, whilst in the south, and in Java and Sumatra, the pickers are busy all year round.

In the highlands, however, tea can only be picked every eight to twelve days, while on the plains it is picked every five to eight days. After four or five years of harvesting, the tea plant needs a break, so it is cut back to its gnarled stem and must start all over again. In this way, tea plants which are up to eighty or one hundred years old, are kept young.

Growing tea: new plants are now usually cultivated by planting cuttings (above and left). The traditional method of growing plants directly from seed (top middle) is now the exception. The plants are pruned regularly (top right) to keep them fresh and at a manageable height for picking. The bushes grow best under the protection of taller trees, as in the tea-garden in China shown on the right.

The journey from fresh green tea-leaf to the brownish-black product sold in the shops is a long one. After the leaves have been "wilted" and rolled, comes the third stage of the process – fermentation (left). Here, the cellular fluid which has been released during the second stage begins to ferment and oxidise. This stage is closely monitored. Afterwards, the leaves are sifted through a sieve.

Processing the Leaves

There are two types of tea, green and black. Both are the result of processing the leaves of the same plant. In the 19th century, people believed differently. "There are two different sorts of tea plant," claimed the widely-read, German *Penny Magazine* in 1833, "brown tea and green tea. Brown tea (*Thea bohea*) grows for several years and reaches a height of five or six feet. As far as we know, it only grows in China and Japan... Green tea (*Thea viridis*) looks like the brown, but its leaves are longer and its flowers have six crown leaves (as opposed to nine in brown tea). Both share the same country of origin."

In the Tea Factory

It is an iron rule that freshly-picked tea-leaves must start being processed within six hours of leaving the field. It has to undergo four processes in the processing plant, which will permit the production of a delicious, aromatic black tea from the tasteless green leaves. These are **wilting**, **rolling**, **fermenting** and **drying**. The fresh leaves are first dried for between eight and twenty-four hours at temperatures of between 25°C and 35°C. This makes them wilt. They are then placed in a thin layer on large wire racks, while ventilators blow warm air over them. The leaves lose much of their natural moisture during this process. A "tea-maker" decides when the leaves are ready, for they must not become too dry or they will break during rolling.

During the second stage, the mechanical rolling of the leaves, the cell-walls of the leaves must be broken down without crushing the leaves themselves. The cellular fluid can then combine with oxygen and the fermentation process can begin. At the same time, fluid containing tannin is squeezed out of the leaves. This stage of the process lasts between thirty and sixty minutes.

The taste and aroma of the tea develops during the next stage of the process – the fermentation. Here, the fluids squeezed out during rolling begin to oxidise and ferment, and help bring about the change in colour and the development of the tea's characteristic aroma. Other chemicals important to the taste of the tea, which are only soluble in very hot water, are also released during fermentation.

The tea is then dried, heated or roasted to help preserve it. The drying stage is part of the fermentation. The tea is dried at a temperature of between 85°C and 100°C for twenty minutes. It is arranged in layers with a different temperature for each layer.

The "raw" tea is then sorted according to leaf size and offered at auction to the agents of the large tea-trading houses. They select samples and air-mail them to their own particular company, where the sample is carefully examined by tea-tasters. The tea-tasters' sensitive taste-buds can soon tell which tea can be used for production and their choice is then telexed to the country of origin of the tea sample.

The Production of Green Tea

Prior to the 19th century, all teas were green. This was because the Chinese produced nothing else. Today, they are still the supreme masters of green tea production, even though they now produce large quantities of black tea. Japan, on the other hand, still produces only green tea.

The tea growers of Taiwan also specialise in producing green tea and partly-fermented Oolong. Most green tea is consumed in the countries where it is produced, although many people in the United States and in North Africa prefer green tea.

Green tea has always been an integral part of the Japanese tea ceremony, whilst in

Europe, it has only recently become more widespread.

Green tea is produced by roasting the fresh leaves at about 100°C in metal containers for a few seconds when they arrive in the factory. This kills off the enzymes in the cells and helps prevent any fermentation. If green tea is prepared with water that has been boiled and then cooled to around 60°C to 70°C, then the taste will not be too sharp or too bitter, despite the tannins still present in the leaf. This process also helps to retain some of the high vitamin C content of the fresh leaf. During the drying stage which immediately follows the roasting, the leaves are frequently picked over and turned by hand, which gives them their dark green colour.

Finally, the leaves are sorted and graded by size. This is the way green tea has been produced in China for many hundreds of years. The Japanese adopted the system, and rationalised and mechanised it, starting with the introduction of two-man machines to harvest the tea. Green tea is thus mass-produced in Japan, with the result that it cannot always compete with the quality of its Chinese equivalent. Partly-fermented Oolong is produced in the same way as black tea, but the fermentation stage is considerably shortened. After it has been dried, it is not sorted according to size, for only whole leaves are used.

The CTC-method

Even the traditional methods of producing tea have been mechanised and automated for many years now, but the so-called CTC-method goes one step further in shortening the stages of production.

The name comes from the three different stages of the process: crushing, tearing and curling. The leaves are rolled (curled) for only a short time, then they are sifted and chopped up. Only then are they fermented. About a quarter of all the tea grown in India is produced using the CTC-method. The result is known as "Broken Tea". Whole-leaf teas cannot be produced by this method, for obvious reasons. For the tea producers, the CTC-method is more economical because both small and large leaves can be used.

Leaf Teas and Broken Teas – the Classification of the Leaf

Many tea packets and price lists bear mysterious abbreviations, sometimes several letters long. They indicate the different classifications of leaf and are, in fact, a general indication of the leaf-size, ranging from the noble leaf to the finest dust used in tea-bags. The dried leaves are sorted by passing them through a sieve. The length of the leaf indicates both place of origin and the quality of the tea. Even under normal weather conditions and in a good harvest, teas from a mountain area such as Darjeeling, or from humid lowlands such as Assam each have their own distinctive aroma.

Of the different technical terms in tea, "Tippy Golden" means that a large proportion of the fine leaves are covered in a light down which has survived the fermentation stage and binds the caramelised cell fluid squeezed out during rolling. "Flowery" means tender, delicate leaves have been picked in blossom, and "Orange" is not the colour, but the regal quality of the tea, so called after the Royal Dutch House of Orange. "Pekoe" was the name originally given to the third leaf picked, and "Souchong", the name given to any further leaves. "Fannings" are the second-smallest leaves used to make tea, "Dust" and "Powdery", the smallest.

The Work of the Tea-taster

The tea-taster is paid for his highly-sensitive taste-buds. His work is to decide which of the 15,000 different teas produced around the world can be sold and used in the popular

*The quality and flavour of a tea are determined by several different factors –
the region where it is grown, good weather conditions before it is harvested,
careful handling during the tea-making process, and the length of time the tea
is then stored. Classification of the leaf is an integral part of the tea-making
process. Mysterious abbreviations can often be found on packets of tea. There
are nine different classes of tea in India, ranging from 1 to 3 for whole leaves,
to between 4 and 9 for broken tea.*

*The four teas pictured here are all from Darjeeling in north-eastern India,
where the favourable mountain climate brings out the full aroma of the tea. At
the back on the left: Fine Tippy Golden Flowery Orange Pekoe 1 (FTGFOP 1 =
Class 1), and at the back on the right: Golden Broken Orange Pekoe (GBOP =
Class 4).*

*The classification of the other two teas is not so elaborate. Front right: Golden
Orange Fannings (GOF) and front left: Special Tippy Tea, a top quality tea
produced in only a few tea-gardens around the world.*

blends of tea. A tea-taster cannot afford to have a cold, for he would not be able to taste the quality of the tea with a "furred" tongue. He should also avoid using tobacco. The taste-buds are most sensitive early in the morning and it is for this reason that the ceremonial tea-tasting sessions take place in the early morning, five times a week. In the sunlit tasting-room, the tools of the tasters are lined up under the window. They consist of white earthenware bowls, white pots and behind each one of them, a tin of tea. Exactly the same amount from every different brand is brewed for exactly the same amount of time – 2.86 grams of tea, with 1/4 litre (8 fl oz) water for exactly five minutes.

The taster dips a small silver spoon into the tea. He slurps it noisily into his mouth (an important part of the process), where his highly-sensitive tongue analyses the taste, and his palate and nose analyse the aroma. Then he quickly spits it out again. He takes another quick glance at the used leaves, and smells them briefly once again, and within three seconds, he has decided whether the tea can be used.

A taster will taste up to three hundred teas a day. The taste tells him where the tea comes from, when it was picked and how it was handled both before and after harvesting. The tea must be tested in this way at six different stages of its production before it can find its way into a blend and sold on the market – before it is purchased in its country of origin, when it is shipped, after it has arrived at its destination, before and after blending, and just before it is packed and distributed. Every tea-drinker benefits from the work of the tea-taster. He guarantees that a particular brand of tea will always taste good. Because the quality of each harvest depends on variable weather conditions and seasons, there are different requirements for each new blend. The customer wants to be able to drink his favourite tea every day of the year, and so a particular brand will consist of over twenty different varieties of tea. It is the job of the taster to decide which varieties will be used.

Right: Statistics covering the biggest tea-producing countries of the world, with production and separate figures for export and import. In 1988 the UK imported 191,542 tonnes of tea, of which 28,843 were re-exported and 162,699 tonnes were consumed domestically. In 1988 the British consumed 2.88 kilograms per head, or 3.77 cups of tea per day for every man, woman and child. Britain imports annually more tea than North America and Europe combined.

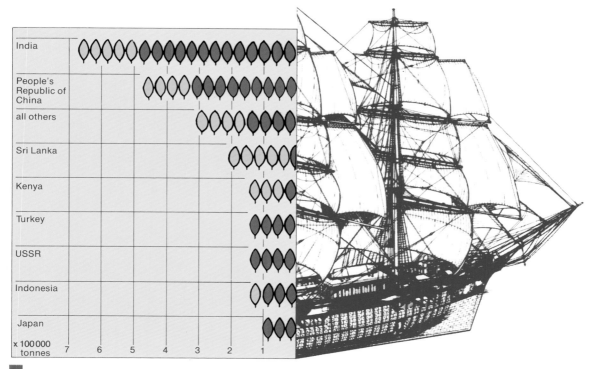

India

People's
Republic of
China

all others

Sri Lanka

Kenya

Turkey

USSR

Indonesia

Japan

x 100 000
tonnes   7   6   5   4   3   2   1

■ Annual Consumption

■ Export

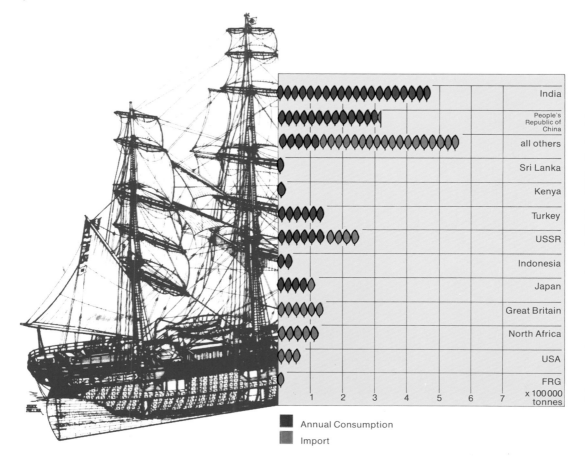

India

People's
Republic of
China

all others

Sri Lanka

Kenya

Turkey

USSR

Indonesia

Japan

Great Britain

North Africa

USA

FRG

    1   2   3   4   5   6   7   x 100 000
tonnes

■ Annual Consumption

■ Import

The Art of Making Tea Today

The correct preparation of tea has always been regarded as something of an art. If this were not the case, then Li Chih-lai, a poet of the Song Dynasty (960–1279 AD), would not have been quite so passionate about the subject. There were three things in this world, he sighed, which caused him most sorrow: "Youth spoilt by false education, beautiful paintings debased by people gawping stupidly at them, and tea squandered by people not knowing the correct way to prepare it."

The tea of the Song Dynasty would probably not suit today's tastes, but that does not alter the problem of how one entices the delicious taste and aroma of tea from a few seemingly inocuous leaves.

Five golden rules, according to the tea authorities of Federal Germany, guarantee the best possible results. Some of these rules still stand today, but new discoveries have since been made which sometimes contradict them.

Rule number 1: Warm the teapot first. Experts have long since abandoned this practice. The longer you pre-warm the pot, the longer it will be before you can enjoy the tea without burning your mouth. The rule can probably be traced back to the time when it was customary to clean a metal pot by rinsing it briefly with hot water immediately before use. It is equally outdated to think that the teapot must not be scrubbed too hard – the thin film which formed on the inside of the pot was said to improve the aroma and the flavour. There is nothing to support this. You may wash the teapot thoroughly, even with washing-up liquid (blasphemous for some tea-lovers). Make sure, however, that you rinse it thoroughly afterwards.

Rule number 2: One teaspoon of tea (or one tea-bag) for every cup. This can be done only when you know exactly how much your teaspoon can hold. The correct amount is between 1.5 g and 2 g of tea for every 150 ml or 200 ml of water. Or, alternatively, 10 g to 12 g of leaf-tea for every litre of water (a little less with broken tea). You can find accurate tea-scales in most good tea shops. If you want to brew even larger amounts of tea, then reduce the quantities by between 15 per cent and 20 per cent. The old custom of one teaspoon for every cup and one "for the pot" has no justification – it was probably merely a strategy of the tea merchants to help them sell more tea.

Rule number 3: Bring fresh water to the boil and pour it over the tea whilst it is still boiling. This is true for black tea. For green tea, you must first let the water cool to between 85°C and 60°C, depending on the type.

You should always have two different pots. One for pouring the water onto the leaves, and another for when the tea has brewed and the leaves are no longer needed. Pots made of glass or porcelain are preferable. Use tap wa-

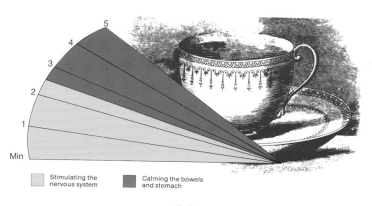

Min

1
2
3
4
5

Stimulating the nervous system

Calming the bowels and stomach

In the first few moments after pouring the water onto the tea, the colour, aroma and contents of the leaves spread slowly and unevenly.

ter, but before filling the kettle in the morning for the first cup, let four or five litres of water run first. This water will be stale and is not suited to tea-making. You can use it to water the flowers. Enquire about the hardness of your water and buy your tea accordingly, but try not to be too fussy – if the water is hard, simply let it boil a little longer. Water from the boiler or from the hot water system is not suitable. You do not need to go as far as Queen Elizabeth II, however, who has her tea water sent to her by jet when she is abroad, or former West German Chancellor Konrad Adenauer, who was said to instruct his chauffeur to collect water from one particular dam near Rhöndorf where he lived.

Rule number 4: Let the tea brew for five minutes. Tea-lovers will know that two or three minutes will suffice for the caffeine to be drawn out of the tea. The longer you let it brew, the more tannins are released into the water, and if it is left for more than five minutes, it will become bitter (see diagram on page 62). Only if the tea is to serve as a sedative, should you let it brew for five minutes. If it is to act as a stimulant, then three minutes will suffice.

Rule number 5: Stir the tea and then pour it into the cups or into a second pot. Cream or milk, granulated or lump sugar can be added to taste. Use a fine-meshed strainer when pouring the tea. The tea in the second pot is ready to drink immediately. If you use a porcelain pot with an internal strainer, you need only remove the strainer. Do not be fooled into buying a tea-infuser made of metal or porcelain, for the leaves will have no room to expand. Tea-machines also cramp the leaves, which can only develop their full strength if they float freely in the water. Filter machines are also not recommended as they will soak up some of the taste, and the colour of the filters is not very appetizing. One more piece of advice: do not keep the tea warm over a candle or spirit lamp after it has been brewed, or it will become stale and cloudy. It is better to brew a fresh pot, with, say, a different type of tea. Neither should you keep it in a thermos flask, for it quickly grows stale through lack of air.

Accompaniments to tea are purely a matter of taste. Granulated sugar is traditional in Central Europe. It improves the flavour and effect of the tea. In East Friesland, a large sugar lump, *kluntje*, is placed in the cup and as it dissolves slowly, it will last for several cups. The English add cold milk, the Frisians cream to their tea, but the tea will become cold and slimy if too much is added and the effect is spoilt. Slices of lemon (traditional in Russia) do nothing to improve the flavour. Neither does a drop of rum which is only excusable if it is the tiniest drop, for it spoils the exquisite taste and aroma of the tea. If you are looking for adventure in your tea-drinking, then you would do better to stick with the aromatic teas of which there are hundreds of different varieties.

The ancient Chinese tradition of a pinch of salt is unnecessary, and it is unlikely that you will season your tea with onions or ginger, or make it more nourishing by adding flour, rice or butter.

A few people do not add anything at all and drink it pure, like the Chinese with their green teas, but once again, that is a matter of taste, for it could very well be that the tea tastes of hay and cow dung, as Liselotte of Pfalz once commented.

The Tea-bag Controversy

It is said that a tea importer from New York invented the tea-bag which contained just the right amount of tea for one cup. He sent samples of the latest harvest in little silk pouches. It made tasting a great deal easier and it probably helped increase his turnover. That was at the beginning of the 20th century. A few years later, a Dresden teashop called *Teekanne* sent portions of tea in small muslin pouches to the troops as part of their tea-ration during World War I. The "tea bomb" was popular with the soldiers, because it allowed them to have a cup of tea at any time, but it was no lasting solution.

Towards the end of the 1920s in America, a tea-bag made of special greaseproof paper was developed. Although, it was a significant step forward, it had a serious disadvantage: the glue used to stick the paper together created an unpleasant aftertaste in the tea.

In 1950, *Teekanne*, the Dresden teashop, which had now moved to the Rhineland, brought out the double-pocketed tea-bag. It consisted of the finest filter paper which had been folded without any glue. The hot water could wash through the leaves from all sides and allow the flavour to develop to its fullest. The double pocketed tea-bag is now used all over the world.

The idea that tea from a tea-bag does not taste as good as tea from a packet is widespread but untrue. Tea-bag tea is selected and blended as carefully as loose tea.

There is good and bad tea in both packets and tea-bags. In both cases, it is best to stick to the well-known brands and take care in choosing exactly what you are putting in your cup.

In fact, tea-bags have a definite advantage – they contain the smallest leaves, known in the trade as "fannings" or "dust". These are the parts of the leaves which have been broken during tea-processing, and as they consist mainly of the tips and edges of the leaves, they contain the highest concentration of the chemicals which give the tea its flavour. Tea from a tea-bag is therefore strongly aromatic and very enjoyable, and has a very strong colour.

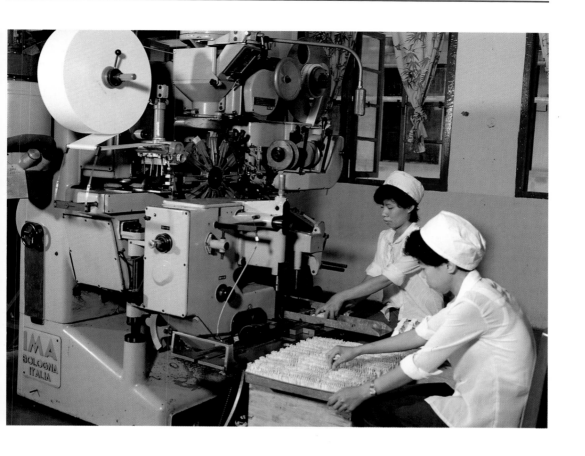

*A tea-bag filling factory in China. More than a quarter of the black tea in the
Federal Republic of Germany is made using tea-bags.*

The Story of Porcelain

Soon after the East India Company had been founded in the Netherlands and the first consignments of tea had started to arrive in Europe, the first porcelain crockery also began to arrive. It was soon discovered that the porcelain acted as an excellent ballast for the tea-ships, and as a result, the porcelain was usually stored at the very bottom of the hold. The tea-chests were then stored in several layers on top. The sale of porcelain soon began to bring in extra money for the trading companies. In 1615, Dutch ships reached Europe with the first 69,057 pieces of porcelain. In his history of Amsterdam written in 1614, Pontanus relates that porcelain had become so commonplace that even the poor were using it. Experts estimate that prior to 1657, Dutch ships had imported at least three million pieces of underglaze blue-decorated porcelain into Europe. A large amount of it would have been used for drinking coffee and cocoa, for tea did not become widespread until about the mid-17th century. But the amount used for tea soon grew and the East India Companies were able to order regular amounts.

In 1644, over 355,800 pieces of porcelain were ordered, including over 100 small teapots, 14,000 octagonal cups and 60,000 teacups in various shapes. In 1780, the figures were 1,134,200 pieces of porcelain, including 450,000 matched cups and saucers, as well as 650 tea-sets and 2,000 tea-caddies.

These huge quantities continued to be imported even after the first porcelain manufactories had been built in Europe, such as the one sponsored by Augustus the Strong in Meissen. A veritable passion for porcelain broke out at all the royal courts. Any castle of importance would now boast a porcelain cabinet with a collection of valuable pieces. Perhaps the most famous one was the collection housed by Augustus the Strong in the "Green Vaults" of his castle in Dresden. Carl Baedecker described the collection as "the most magnificent in the world, which even the collection in the Museum of Sèvres could not outshine". The showpieces of the collection were probably the six-foot dragoon vases which Augustus the Strong had bought in exchange for a regiment of dragoons from Frederick William I of Prussia. The castle at Dresden was destroyed in 1945 and the pieces which survived (including the dragoon vases) are now housed in the museum at Dresden.

Even the less powerful princes and wealthier families took part in the quest for valuable pieces of *chinoiserie*. In the meantime, buyers were no longer satisfied with the designs they were being sent from China. They began to develop their own ideas and sent the drawings and even wooden models of the crockery they wanted to order over to China. These models then had to be returned with the consignments of porcelain, so that those who had commissioned the pieces could check that all their wishes had been respected.

The saucer and the cup handle were European inventions – tea was (and still is) drunk from bowls in China. Different shapes began to be used for the different drinks. Coffee-cups had vertical sides, whilst tea-cups were shaped more like a bowl. Teapots, finger-bowls and tea-caddies all began to conform to European tastes, and their shapes have changed very little since.

Two different types of tea-set were popular at first – the *Solitaire* for one person, or the *Tête-à-tête* for two, and as a rather elegant flourish, the whole thing was served on a matching tray.

Tea was always drunk from the cup. The custom of pouring hot tea into the saucer to let it cool was considered ill-mannered, as was the custom of dipping ("dunking") a biscuit in the tea before eating it. The English would place the teaspoon diagonally across the cup or turn

The Dresden Museum houses the enormous vases which Augustus the Strong of Saxony bought with 600 dragoons from Frederick William I of Prussia in 1717, hence their name – the Dragoon Vases.

the cup upside down on the saucer if they did not want a refill.

It could be embarrassing if you did not know the rules. The Prince de Broglie, for example, drank twelve cups of tea before a friend told him of this traditional "tea-brake".

Another inexperienced foreigner could only stop his cup being constantly refilled by placing his empty cup in his pocket. It is still the custom in East Friesland to place your teaspoon in the cup when you have had enough to drink.

Porcelain is made by firing kaolin, feldspar and quartz in the correct combination at temperatures of up to 1,400°C. The Chinese had perfected this technique in the 13th century, and the white gold was familiar to the Europeans through their trade with China. Nevertheless, porcelain manufacture in Europe went through a number of stages and suffered a number of setbacks. Johann Friedrich Böttger invented a red stoneware in 1707, which when given a high polish would look like porcelain. Above: A teapot made from this material, dating from 1715. In 1708, Böttger, a highly colourful figure with a touch of genius, managed to produce a piece of white porcelain and as a result, the first porcelain factory was founded in Meissen in 1710; it very soon held a complete monopoly.
As a result in the continuing demand for expensive porcelain, Europe continued to import large quantities from China. Right: Tea-caddies of porcelain made in China to suit European tastes.

The Gsheli region is only 30 miles from Moscow. It is rich in China clay, and famous since the 14th century for its manufacture of ceramics. The heyday of Gshelimajolica came around 1670. Master craftsmen created pots decorated with sculptural reliefs, and bowls for kumyss (fermented mares' milk), teapots, sugar bowls and vases.
This china, which is still popular today, is easily recognisable by the deep-blue hand painting.

71

Tea and Health

From the very beginning, there has always been a lively debate as to the medicinal qualities of tea. The Swedish King Gustav III (1746–1792) conducted a famous experiment to see whether tea or coffee were more beneficial to health. The King allowed two robbers and murderers who had been sentenced to death to be used as guinea-pigs in an experiment. They were each given thirty cups a day to drink, one of coffee, the other of tea. Two eminent professors were to conduct the experiment. The results, however, were poor. First one professor died, then the other. The King was assassinated in 1792 and the two guinea-pigs went on to live to a ripe old age.

The Effects of Tea

Tea has a stimulating effect on a man's intellectual capacities. This can be traced to the caffeine content of the drink. The young leaves are rich in polyphenols (tannins), which are responsible for the flavour and colour of the drink.

Caffeine was first isolated in a pure form from coffee beans by Friedlieb Ferdinand Runge in 1820. In 1827, a Frenchman named Oudry discovered an unknown substance in tea-leaves which he called tannin. In 1837, however, Gerard J. Mulder showed that tannin was identical to caffeine.

Caffeine is released almost immediately from the leaves into boiling water. The polyphenols, however, are released much more slowly. This can be seen in the gradual deepening of the colour but also in the slightly bitter flavour of tea which has been brewed for too long.

After drinking tea, the concentration of caffeine in the blood is almost the same as after drinking coffee, but the effects of caffeine vary according to whether you have drunk a cup of tea or a cup of coffee. This is probably a result of the other elements in the drink – the polyphenols in tea, or the products of roasting in coffee.

Tea contains a higher percentage of caffeine than does coffee, but a pound of tea gives many more cups than a pound of coffee. A cup of tea will therefore contain only 0.053 grams of caffeine, whilst a cup of coffee will contain 0.1 grams.

The caffeine in tea has a slower, longer-lasting effect than the caffeine in coffee. The caffeine in tea affects the central nervous system, whilst the caffeine in coffee affects only the heart. Tea stimulates but does not excite. It can be scientifically proven that tea improves performance. The old method used as proof was to have the experimentees add up rows of figures. The computer addition test works in the same way. More recently, however, performance has been judged by a test in which balls of varying sizes must be thrown into a rotating cylinder with slits cut into the sides. After the highest score has been ascertained, it is compared to scores attained after drinking tea. The task was completed with twenty-five per cent fewer mistakes and in three-quarters of the time after drinking tea. Apart from the alkaloid caffeine, which is a xanthin, tea contains smaller amounts of other substances related to caffeine, such as theophylline and theobromine.

The **tannins** contained in tea (catechines) soothe the bowels and stomach. If you want to increase their effect then you should let the tea stand for five minutes or more, or drink green tea which has higher concentrations of these chemicals. The tannic acid also helps counteract the effect of the caffeine. Chemists do not like to talk of tannic acid or tannins, they prefer the name "polyphenols" as opposed, say, to oak bark which is used to tan leather.

The main component of the polyphenols is epigallocatechingallate (EGCG). According

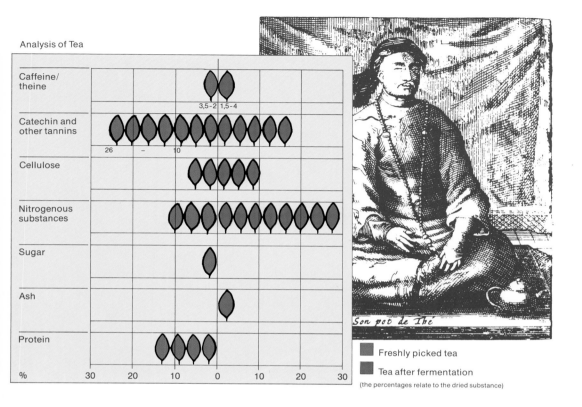

Analysis of Tea

Caffeine/theine	3,5-2	1,5-4
Catechin and other tannins	26	10
Cellulose		
Nitrogenous substances		
Sugar		
Ash		
Protein		

% 30 20 10 0 10 20 30

Freshly picked tea

Tea after fermentation

(the percentages relate to the dried substance)

Son pot de Thé

to a report in *Geo* magazine, in November, 1987, Japanese scientists discovered through experiments on animals that EGCG can help to prevent cancer, especially cancers of the gullet, stomach and bowels. It is found mainly in green tea. Fermentation reduces it in black tea. Two new catechines were discovered a few years ago during research into polyphenols at the Institute for Human Nutrition and Food Science at the University of Kiel. These scientists also discovered new facts about the enzymes involved in the development of flavour during fermentation.

Tea also contains **minerals**, such as potassium and fluorine, as well as copper, iron, manganese and nickel. Fluorine is perhaps the most interesting, for it helps protect teeth from decay. The effect of the amino-acid theanin, also contained in tea, is currently being investigated. It probably regulates the amount of nitrogen in the tea plant. In Japan, it has been

established that theanin slows down the effects of caffeine on the body.

Tea is also a good source of **vitamins**, including some from the vitamin B complex, which are good for the nerves and for fighting stress. Vitamin B is also essential for growth. The vitamin C content is high in the fresh leaf (four times as high as in lemon juice) but it is greatly reduced during fermentation and is destroyed altogether when the tea is brewed. Vitamins E2, P and K strengthen the capillary walls and make the skin more elastic. Lovers of **green tea** are keen to emphasise its health-giving properties, and these claims have now been supported by numerous studies undertaken by scientists in China, Japan and the USSR.

This is because the processing of green tea destroys a fewer number of tannins and a smaller amount of vitamin C than does the processing of black tea. There are substances

Nettle   Ribwort   Camomile   Elderflowers   Whitehorn
Coltsfoot   Lime blossoms   Hops

The following selection is not extensive, but is only meant as a guide. We have restricted ourselves to the following questions: What is available? How long must the leaves or other parts of the plants remain in boiling water? Which herb tea is useful against which ailment? To what further uses can other parts of the plant be put? Is it possible to grow the plant at home?

Nettle: Leaves can be picked between April and May, the roots between May and July. Let the tea brew for eight or ten minutes. It is useful against rheumatism, gout, ailments of the stomach, the pancreas and the urinary tract. The leaves can also be used in tinctures for burns, sunburn and insect bites, and when they are very young, they can even be eaten as a vegetable. They cannot and need not be grown domestically.

Coltsfoot: The flowers can be picked without the stems in spring, or the leaves in early summer. The tea needs to brew for about ten minutes. Use it for catarrh of the throat, hoarseness and bronchitis. It cannot be grown indoors.

Ribwort: The leaves can be picked and dried in spring, the ripe seeds between August and October. Leave the tea to brew for ten minutes; it helps combat bronchial catarrh, phlegmy coughs, fevers and upset stomach. An extract from the seeds is good for stabilising the bowels and the juice of the fresh leaves helps heal wounds. As ribwort grows so easily in the wild, you do not need to grow it in the home.

Camomile: Pick the flowers on the third and fifth days after they have blossomed, between May and September.

Let the tea brew for ten minutes. It is particularly helpful in combatting gastritis, cystitis, inflammation of the bowels, mouth and throat. It can also be used in poultices and baths for inflammation of the skin and the mucous membrane. It can be grown in window-boxes, flower pots and in the garden.

Elderflowers: The flowers can be picked after they have blossomed in June and July. The tea must brew for ten minutes and is good for sweating out fevers, cleansing the blood, and because of its high vitamin C content, it is very refreshing. Elderflower water is an excellent astringent for the face, and an infusion of the leaves will kill garden pests. Elder can be grown in the garden.

Lime (Linden) blossoms (summer and winter limes): Lime blossoms between June and July. A tea brewed for ten minutes from the flowers is good for sweating out infections and colds, for calming the nerves, and for cleansing the blood. Limewood charcoal helps combat for diarrhoea. A lot of patience is required to grow lime trees at home. Elderflowers and lime blossoms are frequently used together.

Whitehorn: The flowers in April, the berries in autumn and the leaves all year round produce a tea which should be left to brew for ten to twenty minutes. It is good for a weak or nervous heart, and for high and low blood pressure. Concentrated whitehorn is used medicinally and grows well in the garden.

Hops: A tea can be made from the flowers of the plant shortly before they reach maturity between May and July. When it is brewed for ten minutes it helps counteract loss

| | Fennel | (Lemon) Balm | | Sage | Rosehip |
| Peppermint | | Common yarrow | Hollyhock | Wormwood | |

of appetite and sleeplessness. Their use in brewing beer is well-known, but it is less well-known that they can be cultivated successfully as a garden plant.

Fennel: Seeds can be gathered and dried between August and September. Let the tea brew for ten minutes. It aids digestion, especially in young babies. It is a good expectorant and helps against loss of appetite. The leaves can be used as a herb; another type of fennel can be eaten as a vegetable. It is easy to grow in the garden.

(Lemon) Balm: Leaves should be picked shortly before blossom in July and August. The tea should brew for ten to fifteen minutes, and is good against weakness, problems of the heart, bowels and stomach, and in case of convulsions. The leaves taste good in salads, sauces and soups. Lemon balm is grown widely in gardens, and is often used in combination with peppermint.

Sage: The leaves should be picked just before the herb flowers between June and July. When brewed for five or ten minutes, it produces a very pleasant tea. It reduces sweating, as well as inflammation of the gums and the throat. Tincture of sage can be dabbed on insect bites and added to hot foot-baths. It can be grown in window-boxes, flowerpots and in the garden.

Peppermint: The peppermint leaves should be used just before flowering between the months June and August. Let the peppermint tea brew for five or ten minutes in boiling hot water. It is effective against convulsions and irritation of the stomach, the gall and the bowels. If watered regularly, it can be grown easily in window-boxes, flowerpots and in the garden.

Common yarrow: Should be picked when flowering, between June and September. The herb should be brewed for twenty minutes to produce a tea which contains chemicals to stimulate stomach, gall, bowels, kidneys and blood circulation. The same chemicals also help stop nosebleeds. The plant does not need to be grown domestically as it can be found very easily in the wild.

Hollyhock: The flowers must be picked shortly after they open between July and September. If only the hollyhock is used, brew it for fifteen minutes, but if a combination of aniseed and fennel is also used, brew for only ten minutes. It is good for catarrh of the stomach and the bowels, stomach ulcers and catarrh in the upper air passages. Externally, it can be used for small cuts and scratches. It cannot be grown domestically.

Wormwood: The leaves and the tips of branches should be picked just before they flower between July and September. The tea should be very diluted – one teaspoon for every litre of water – and should be brewed for ten minutes. It contains substances which stimulate the mucous membrane in the mouth, the stomach, the gall and the liver. Crushed leaves can be used to staunch bleeding of wounds. It is possible to grow wormwood in the garden.

Rosehip: The chopped skins of the autumnal fruit, minus stems and seeds, should be boiled for ten minutes. The seeds can be left to brew on their own for twenty minutes in hot water. Rosehip tea is good for fighting ailments of the gall, kidneys and bladder and for cleansing the blood. It can be grown in the garden or in flowerpots.

in green tea which are quick and effective in staunching haemorrhages of the brain, stomach and intestines. Infections such as dysentery and ailments such as high blood pressure, hardening of the arteries, rheumatism and hepatitis have all been successfully combatting by administering strong green tea. Apart from its medicinal properties, green tea tastes good, once one has become accustomed to its bitterness.

Some varieties have a sweet aftertaste even without any sugar or sweetener. This is because the tannins in the tea stimulate the salivary glands. All in all, green tea is a drink which requires a more refined sense of taste than black tea or coffee.

It is unclear what effect the chlorophyll contained in tea has on the body. Finally, there are the ethers peculiar to tea which give the tea its taste and are probably stimulants like caffeine. Tea has practically no calories and is therefore suitable for dieting if drunk without any milk or sugar. Artificial sweeteners can be added.

Herb Teas

Herb teas have been used for medicinal purposes throughout Europe from the earliest times. It was during the 19th century, however, that the majority of people began to drink them for pleasure, because they could not afford the imported green and black teas. Country folk, in particular, drank teas made from sage, speedwell, willow and birch leaves, because these could be gathered very easily. Only in the first few years of the 20th century did town-dwellers begin to drink herb teas, and very recently, there has been a great upsurge in interest in a wide variety of different teas. People drink them either because they are good for the health or help in relaxation. The preparation of almost all herb teas is very easy and varies little from one tea to another. Just follow the instructions on the packets. If you want to pick the herbs yourself, you will need to have an extensive knowledge of

botany and ecology. For instance, you will need to know which areas are free from harmful substances such as weedkillers and the right time to harvest the herbs, and you will need to be familiar with the nature conservation laws, as well as a great deal more. Once you know all this, you will be able to grow many herbs at home, and follow in the tradition of the famous herbalists' gardens.

The selection of herb teas should whet your appetite, and supplement the following recipes. Of course, we cannot guarantee that the teas will have the desired effect. If symptoms of illness persist, you should consult a doctor as soon as possible.

Enough of all this theory!

On the following pages, you will find a number of ideas for serving tea and a few extra suggestions to make your tea-table look even more inviting.

Naturally, most of the following recipes are for drinks and many use the three different concentrations of tea outlined on the right.

Before turning to the recipes, we would like to give you a little tip on sweetness. The lump sugar referred to in the recipes is traditional loaf sugar, which is very hard to obtain in English-speaking countries. Lump sugar, preferably cane sugar, has been substituted, but it will dissolve far more quickly. You can also substitute plain boiled sweets. The quantities of sugar in the recipes can be reduced by between 20 per cent and 40 per cent according to taste or to the character of the wine or any other drink you might be blending with it. However, as far as the cake and pastry recipes are concerned, you must ensure that the dough retains the right consistency when smaller quantities of sugar are used. Always use half the required amount if honey is used instead of sugar.

As far as measurements are concerned, the metric measurement is followed first by the British (imperial) measure and then by the

Basic recipe for different concentrations of tea:
Normal strength: 1 1/4–1 1/2 teaspoons per 1/4 litre (9 fl oz / 1 cup)
= 2.5–3 g loose tea or a maximum of 2 x 1.5 g tea-bags.
Strong tea: 2 1/2 teaspoons per 1/4 litre (9 fl oz / 1 cup)
= 4–5 g or 3 x 1.5–1.75 g tea-bags.
Extra strong tea or tea essence: 3–3 1/2 teaspoons
per 1/4 litre (9 fl oz / 1 cup) = 6–7 g or 4 x 1.5–1.75 g tea-bags.
When calculating for larger quantities such as 1 litre (1 3/4 pints / 1 quart),
simply multiply by four.

American cup measurement, all rounded up for convenience.
We leave the choice for the different types of tea and all the extras up to you. Our recipes are there to ensure that they taste good – all you need to do is sit back and enjoy the fine aroma of the teas, the cocktails, punches, desserts and other titbits. Bon Appétit!

Madrid Pineapple Tea

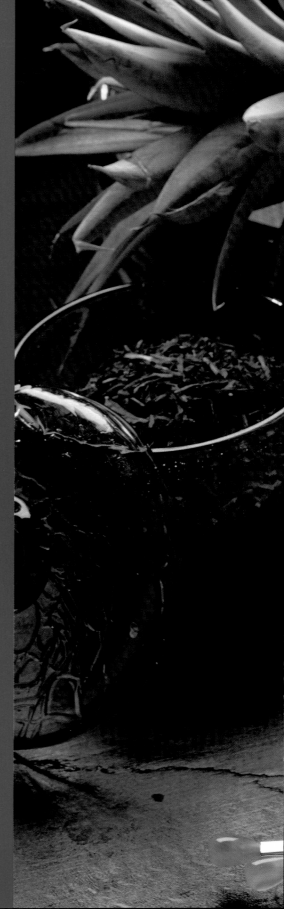

Pineapple, the main ingredient in this recipe, is one of the most important tropical fruits in modern cuisine. Eight million tonnes are harvested worldwide every year. The first European to see the fruit was Christopher Columbus, and the Spaniards and Portuguese then introduced it to the Old World. The Portuguese gave the fruit its name from the language of the Tupi-Guarani, the islanders who then inhabited the West Indies. They called the pineapple *nana meant*, meaning "precious fruit"; *Abacaxi*, or "spikey fruit", is another native name for the pineapple. English is practically the only European language that does not use the adapted name *ananas* coined by the Portuguese. Most of our pineapples (which grow on bushes rather than trees) are produced in the Ivory Coast; the relatively short voyage means that they may be shipped almost peak ripeness, since pineapples do not ripen further after picking.

1 can pineapple chunks
8 tablespoons rum
1/2 litre (18 fl oz / 2 cups) water
8 teaspoons black tea
4 tablespoons sugar
ice cubes

Drain the pineapple and soak it in the rum for 3–4 hours. Bring water to the boil and make the tea. Let it brew for 3–4 minutes, then pour it out and add sugar to taste. Drop ice cubes into four glasses, divide the rum and pineapple chunks between them and top up with the hot tea.

Georgian Beekeeper's Tea

Georgia is a fertile land that yields rich harvests of fruit and vegetables, besides being the Soviet Union's most important tea-growing region. Honey is widely used as a sweetener and forms the basis of many traditional sweet dishes, of which *gosinaki* is a typical example. It is made from honey, nuts and icing sugar.

In terms of its cuisine, Georgia is perhaps the least-known of all Soviet regions and therefore offers some unacknowledged gems. For example, take this recipe for spit-roasted ox, which caters for the Georgians' huge appetites. The ox is stuffed with a freshly slaughtered calf, which is in turn stuffed with a lamb. The lamb is stuffed with a turkey which contains a goose stuffed with a duck. The final morsel is a chicken shoe-horned into the duck. Herbs and spices are blended to give each layer its particular character.

60 cl (1 pint / 2 2/3 cups) strong tea essence
100 g (4 oz / 1/2 cup) liquid honey
20 cl (7 fl oz / 3/4 cup) vodka
1 teaspoon vanilla sugar

Prepare the tea using about 6 or 7 teaspoons of loose tea to a pint or so of water, then simmer in a pan with honey and vodka, stirring constantly. Remove the pan from the heat, add vanilla sugar and serve immediately in heat-resistant glasses.

Fruit-tea Cup

Strawberry punch is an old favourite, but for a change try this exotic variation. Use canned fruit, because the canning syrup provides the necessary sweetness along with the lump sugar. Lychees, the fruit of a sapindaceous tree, were known to the ancient Chinese, who considered them the finest fruit of all. Mauritius and Madagascar are the most common sources of fresh lychees, although the South African crop becomes available in February. Their flavour is difficult to pin down, but falls somewhere between a grape and a sour cherry, with slight overtones of nutmeg.

1 can lychees
1 can figs
1 can loquats or mangoes
250 g (9 oz / 1 3/4 cups) sultanas
20 g (3/4 ounce) lump sugar
1 bottle (70 cl / 1 1/4 pints / 3 cups)
brandy
3 litres (5 1/4 pints / 3 quarts) water
4 tablespoons each of black tea,
orange tea and mango tea
10 drops angostura bitters

Combine the fruit with its juice or syrup, the sultanas, the lump sugar and the brandy in a basin and allow to stand for about 6 hours. Bring the water to the boil. Combine the teas and pour the water over them; let the tea brew for 4–5 minutes. Strain off the tea and leave it to cool, then refrigerate until chilled. Pour the tea over the fruit and add angostura to taste.

Summer Fruit Cup

This summery recipe is very adaptable. You can pick and choose your type of fruit or add extra alcohol with dashes of gin, calvados or kirsch. Choose wines that are not too dry to avoid a bitter result. Additional sugar will help to regulate this.

A well-blended punch is unique as a drink that both refreshes and stimulates, as well as helping parties go with a swing, yet not leaving guests with a thick head. The best results can only be achieved by applying care, understanding and experience. Use a wine of a reasonable quality – not necessarily the very finest, but at the same time, not the poorest.

1 litre (1 3/4 pints / 1 quart) chilled
black tea
125 g (5 oz) fresh strawberries
125 g (5 oz) peaches
2–3 tablespoons sugar
1 bottle red wine
1 bottle sparkling white wine

Prepare a strong brew of tea then leave to cool. Hull the strawberries then cut into quarters. Blanch the peaches by dipping them briefly in boiling water. Remove the stones, peel and slice thinly. Place all the fruit together in the punch-bowl and sprinkle with sugar before covering with wine and tea.

Frisian Buttercake

No special skill is needed to prepare this dough.

For the dough:
500 g (1 1/4 lbs / 4 cups) flour
30 g (1 oz) yeast
1/4 litre (8 fl oz / 1/2 cup) lukewarm milk
75 g (3 oz / 1/3 cup) sugar
100 g (4 oz / 1/2 cup) butter
1 teaspoon salt
grated rind of 1/2 unsqueezed lemon
pinch of mace
butter to grease tin (pan)
For the topping:
75 g (3 oz / 1/3 cup) butter
125 g (5 oz / 2/3 cup) sugar
1 packet vanilla sugar
1/2 teaspoon ground cinnamon
100 g (4 oz / 1 cup) ground almonds
1/8 litre (4 fl oz / 1/2 cup) sour cream

To make the dough, sift 125 g (4 oz / 1 cup) of the flour into a basin and make a well in the centre. Crumble the yeast into the hollow with a teaspoon of the sugar, and add a small quantity of milk. Stir until the mixture is of a creamy consistency. Cover lightly with a damp muslin cloth and leave to rise away from draughts for at least 30 minutes. Add the rest of the dough ingredients and knead thoroughly; best results are achieved using the dough hook on an electric mixer. Cover with a cloth again and leave to rise for a further half hour. Then roll out the dough and lay it on a greased baking sheet (tray). Leave to rise for a further 20 minutes. Prick the dough all over with a fork. To make the topping, melt the butter and brush it over the top of the dough. Sprinkle with the sugar, vanilla sugar, cinnamon and almonds and spread the cream evenly over the top. Bake for 25–30 minutes at 410–450 °F (200–220 °C). Tastes superb straight from the oven.

Tea Cocktail with Bananas

The banana is one of the oldest plants to be cultivated by man. Indian and Buddhist texts first mention it some six centuries before Christ. The yellow bananas so familiar to us are largely chosen for their ease of transport. They are shipped in their unripe state and subsequently ripened before sale. Greenish-yellow, orange and violet bananas also exist, however. The fruit is rich in vitamins A, E and U as well as minerals such as phosphorous, copper, iron, manganese, zinc and iodine. Bananas are full of energy, 100 g yields 90 kcal/376 kJ. Because bananas are so easily digested, remaining in the stomach for only 110 minutes on average, they are recommended for babies, the elderly and for many special dietary requirements. Their salt content is the lowest of all fruits.

2 bananas
6 cl (4 tablespoons) banana liqueur
4 cl (3 tablespoons) brandy
1/2 litre (18 fl oz / 2 cups) water
5 teaspoons black tea
50 g (2 oz / 1/4 cup) lump sugar
6 drops angostura bitters

Peel and slice the bananas, then leave to soak for 2–3 hours in the brandy and banana liqueur. Boil the water and pour over the tea and lump sugar, leaving for 4–5 minutes before straining off and chilling. Finally, pour tea over bananas, add the angostura and divide the cocktail between 4 glasses.

Tea Cocktail with Figs

Fresh figs come from Italy and Brazil, as well as being supplied in dried form or as tinned preserves from several Mediterranean countries. "The fig is a poem among fruit", wrote the epicure Baron Eugen von Vaerst in 1851. "Anyone who has sampled the small figs of Greece can well understand the great delight that the gourmets of Athens took in that fruit." The fig was first recorded in the Aegean in the second millennium BC. According to the Greeks, the art of drying figs was discovered by the goddess Cybele. The flavour of tea is perfectly complemented by the sweet aromatic fruit, which is a source of vitamin A, calcium and iron.

1 can figs
1/8 litre (4 fl oz / 1/2 cup) vodka
4 cl (3 tablespoons) brandy
1/2 litre (18 fl oz / 2 cups) water
5 teaspoons black tea
50 g (2 oz / 1/4 cup) lump sugar
6 drops angostura bitters

Drain the figs but retain the juice, then allow them to soak for 5–6 hours in the vodka and brandy mixture. Boil the water and brew the tea for 4 minutes before stirring in the lump sugar. Stir until it has completely dissolved. Chill the tea, then combine it with the fig juice and pour over the fruit. Divide the cocktail between 4 glasses.

"Trópicos Furiosos" Tea Cocktail

The choice of tropical fruit in this recipe is up to you. Figs, kiwis, papaya and mango are all recommended, as is pineapple. Use a demi-sec sparkling white wine to avoid the need to add sugar.

Here it is worth remembering a few elementary rules that apply to all cold drinks. Don't worry about trying new combinations, but take care not to go overboard. If your creation tastes like something out of the slops bucket, your guests will soon be heading for the door. Also, too much sugar causes the drink to lose its power as a thirst-quencher. Finally, remember to serve well-chilled, but without ice cubes unless specifically called for by the recipe, as in the case of original iced tea.

1/2 litre (18 fl oz / 2 cups) strong chilled tea
2 cl (1 1/2 tablespoons) rum
2 cl (1 1/2 tablespoons) gin
250 g (9 oz / 1 cup) thinly sliced fresh figs, kiwis, papaya or mango
1 bottle sparkling white wine

Prepare a strong brew of tea and allow to chill before mixing with rum and gin. Divide the fruit between 4 glasses, cover with tea mixture and top up with the sparkling wine.

Tea Cocktail with Vermouth

Tea is perfect in combination with exotic fruits. This recipe uses lychees or loquats. The former were originally Chinese, as were the less well-known loquats. These are grown chiefly in Japan, but also in Brazil and Spain where most of our fresh and tinned loquats are produced. They are also known as Japanese medlars and grow to the size of a plum; loquats are similar in colour to apricots, taste sweetly aromatic and have a refreshing acid content. Botanists know them as *Eriobotrya japonica*.

1 small can lychees or loquats
1/8 litre (4 fl oz / 1/2 cup) dry white vermouth
1/2 litre (18 fl oz / 2 cups) water
5 teaspoons black tea
50 g (2 oz / 1/4 cup) lump sugar
1/4 litre (8 fl oz / 1 cup) orange juice

Drain the fruit but reserve the juice. Soak the lychees or loquats in vermouth and allow to stand for 5–6 hours. Boil the water, pour it over the tea and lump sugar and allow to brew for 4–5 minutes. Strain off tea and leave to cool. Finally, blend the tea and fruit juice, pour over fruit and serve chilled.

Curaçao Tea Grog

Everyone knows the recipe for a real sailor's grog. Rum, yes. Sugar, maybe. Water? Never. This wintry recipe is far removed from the original, but no less of a treat. The story of grog began like this. In 1745, Admiral Vernon of the British Navy applied his mind to the problem of reducing the prodigious consumption of rum aboard His Majesty's sailing ships by weaning the men off the hard stuff. Though at the time no specific name was given to the drink, the result was grog – watered rum with added sugar. Because the Admiral was fond of parading in a cloak of silk and camelhair, known as *grogram*, the sailors dubbed him "Old Grog", and since they soon came to despise his watered rum it was soon named "grog" in turn.

1/2 litre (18 fl oz / 2 cups) water
4 teaspoons black tea
1–2 teaspoon sugar
1/8 litre (4 fl oz / 1/2 cup) Curaçao
8 cl (5 tablespoons) rum
4 slices of lemon
4 cloves

Boil the water and brew the tea for 3–4 minutes. Mix with the other ingredients and pour into grog glasses (re-heat over a low flame if necessary). Drop a clove and a slice of lemon into each glass before serving.

Iced Tea

Far from being merely cold tea, this is a traditional recipe with its own story. At the 1904 World's Fair in St. Louis, USA, the Englishman Richard Blechynden was in charge of a stand hired by a group of tea merchants. Because the Americans were used to green China tea, it was his job to introduce them to the black blends from India, of which he had a decent number on display. Unfortunately St. Louis was enjoying a heat wave at the time and the demand was exclusively for cold drinks. Blechynden suddenly struck on the idea of boosting his flagging trade by pouring freshly-brewed tea over ice cubes and serving it to the gasping public. The idea was an immediate hit that soon spread to every corner of the United States.

1 litre (1 3/4 pints / 1 quart) water
10−12 teaspoons black tea
sugar and lemon juice to taste
ice cubes

Prepare a good strong brew, then strain it and add sugar and lemon juice. Drop 2 or 3 ice cubes into tall glasses and pour the hot tea directly over them. Rapid cooling preserves all the properties of the tea – as well as its aroma, taste and colour.

Indian Spiced Tea

Spiced tea is perhaps a predictable Indian speciality. No other country on earth produces
such a variety of spices. There are very few
exotic spices that cannot be obtained from Indian soil. Black pepper, ginger, cardamom,
cloves, chilis, cinnamon, nutmeg, mace,
cumin, aniseed, caraway, coriander, fennel
and celery seeds are among the best-known
products. Curry powder as found in European
shops has little in common with the powder
pounded, ground and blended fresh every day
for use in Indian kitchens. The variations
known to the average Indian cook would not
occur to most of us in our wildest dreams.

3/4 litre (26 fl oz / 3 cups) water
6 teaspoons black tea
1 pinch ground cardamom
1/4 teaspoon ground aniseed
3 cloves
1/4 cinnamon stick

Boil the water and pour it over the tea. Add
the spices. Allow to brew for 4 to 5 minutes
before pouring. It is customary for this type of
tea to be served with milk and sugar. Candied
fruit can also be served.

Hunter's Tea

There is no end of drinks for keeping things lively in ski-lodges. Having considerable alcohol content means they tend to be fairly potent since they usually follow pretty liberal recipes. Rum, kirsch and brandy tend to be mixed at will. The same is broadly true of Hunter's Tea (Jagertee), which is served to a different recipe in every mountain retreat in the Tyrol. "Ich trinke Jagertee, bis ich nix mehr seh" ("I drink Hunter's Tea till I can no longer see") is the general approach. Some of these drinks dispense with the tea element altogether, like "Tuxer Tee" which is made with kirsch, pale rum, butter and sugar, or the "Liftwärmer" prepared with dry white wine, rum, lemons and sugar. "Wolpertinger" is a distant relative of Jagertee named after a mythical beast said to live in the Bavarian Alps. Use 1/8 litre (4 fl oz / 1/2 cup) of strong hot tea, 1 1/2 tablespoons of whisky and some ground cardamom. The tea is topped with sweet whipped cream.

For one person:
1/8 litre (4 fl o z / 1/2 cup) hot black tea
1 dash each of white wine, kirsch and rum
lump sugar

Brew the tea in the usual way, then add the rest of the ingredients and warm it gently, but do not allow to boil. Drop the sugar in at the same time, and serve piping hot in a heat-resistant glass or mug.

Redcurrant Tea

This recipe uses a clever trick that gives a new dimension to iced teas; try it out on a warm summer evening. The key is in the redcurrant juice which should be frozen into cubes in advance. If you want to experiment there is any amount of room to manoeuvre, using different fruit juices. Red- white- and blackcurrant juice is rich in minerals and vitamins and very acid. Half a litre (18 fl oz / 2 cups) contains 1050 kJ or 25 kcal. You can also substitute cranberry juice, which is rich in vitamin C and as beautifully coloured as redcurrant juice. The lemons must be untreated so you may have to look beyond your greengrocer to obtain them without a treated rind.

For 6 servings:
1/2 litre (18 fl oz / 2 cups) redcurrant juice
1 litre (1 3/4 pints / 1 quart) water
6 teaspoons black tea
sugar to taste
1 lemon or redcurrants for garnish

Freeze the redcurrant juice into cubes. Brew the tea, sweeten, strain and leave to cool. Drop 2 or 3 redcurrant cubes into each glass and top up with the cooled tea. Slit the sliced lemon to fit over the rim of the glasses or garnish with redcurrants before serving.

Cardamom Tea

Coffee or tea prepared with cardamom pods is a speciality of the Near and Far East. The spice promotes good digestion and regulates the stomach; it is also apocryphally claimed to boost male potency. India is one of the largest producers of cardamom, most of which is sold on the home market. As well as being used in tea, known in India as *ilaichi chah*, it also goes into the preparation of betel. The Arabs prefer cardamom in its green state; Indian and Guatemalan growers needed to perfect a new drying process to satisfy this demand.

10 green cardamom pods
1 1/2 litres (2 1/2 pints /
1 1/2 quarts) water
3 tablespoons black tea
1 segment unsqueezed lemon or
orange peel
fresh milk and sugar

Drop cardamom pods into water and bring to the boil, then leave pods to steep for 5 minutes or so over a low flame. Remove the pan from heat and allow to steep for a further 10 minutes. Put tea and citrus into a teapot, bring the cardamom back to the boil and pour the liquid over the tea, leaving to brew for 3 minutes before serving with milk and sugar.

Kiwi Ice-cream Tea

The number of recipes using kiwi fruit runs into the hundreds. It is recommended with salads, for breakfast, as an ingredient of soup and garnish for meat dishes. Here it is used as a refreshing ingredient in a drink.

Of all exotic fruit, the kiwi can boast the most dynamic career; within just a few years it had become *the* fruit to have on one's table. Though first records indicate that it existed in 15th-century China, it was a New Zealander who renamed the Chinese gooseberry after his national bird, the flightless kiwi, and launched it on its mission of world conquest.

1/2 litre (18 fl oz / 2 cups) water
2 teaspoons black tea
2 teaspoons peppermint tea
8 small scoops lemon ice-cream
2 large kiwi fruits
2 cl (1 1/2 tablespoons) peppermint liqueur

Prepare the black tea and peppermint tea separately using half the water for each. Allow to brew, then pour off and blend the liquids before chilling. Peel and liquidize the kiwis, then add ice-cream and liqueur. Divide between 4 glasses and top up with ice-cold tea.

Frisian "Knüppeltorte"

An excellent complement to Frisian tea – the individual fritters of which the cake consists are known as *Knüppel*.

Fritter batter:
6 egg yolks
1/8 litre (4 fl oz / 1/2 cup) sour cream
100 g (4 oz / 1/2 cup) sugar
150 g (6 oz / 1 1/2 cups) flour
75 g (3 oz / 1/3 cup) butter
butter for the tin
Filling:
100 g (4 oz / 1/2 cup) chopped candied orange peel
200–300 g (8–12 oz / 1 3/4 cups) sugar
juice of 2 lemons
250 g (9 oz / 1 cup) ground almonds
1 packet vanilla sugar
1 tablespoon rum
whipped cream to garnish

To make the batter, whisk the egg yolks with the sour cream. Gradually add sugar and flour to form a stiff batter. Heat butter in a frying-pan (skillet). Use a tablespoon to drop lumps of the batter about 6 cm / 2 1/2 inches in diameter into the hot butter. Fry until crisp and brown both sides. Drain on brown paper. To make the filling, chop the candied peel finely. Dissolve the sugar in the lemon juice, then stir in the almonds, vanilla sugar, rum and candied peel. Butter a 10-cm / 8-inch round cake tin (pan). Arrange a layer of fritters on the bottom, and spread it with some of the filling. Arrange alternate layers of fritters and filling until both filling and fritters are used up, finishing with a layer of fritters. Refrigerate overnight. Turn out of the tin shortly before serving. To serve, slice into segments and garnish with whipped cream.

Persian Love Potion

This spiced oriental tea is closely related to Indian spiced tea. You might choose to add granulated or lump sugar if you find it too powerful. Persia (modern day Iran) is not a large producer of spices, with the exception of caraway seed; the Persians actually have to rely on Indian or Indonesian imports. This is not to say that Iranian cooking lacks spice, in fact, quite the contrary. The European mind can quite easily conjure up a vision of this love potion being drunk in the secret surroundings of a harem. Though it lacks alcohol, which is banned under Islamic law, the addition of rum, brandy or kirsch is an ideal way to give the potion some extra zip.

3/4 litre (26 fl oz / 3 cups) water
6 teaspoons black tea
1 pinch ground ginger
1 pinch ground cinnamon
1 clove
4 glacé cherries or pineapple chunks

Boil the water, pour it over the tea and add the spices immediately. Allow to brew for 4–5 minutes before straining. Serve with cherries or pineapple chunks.

Mango Tea Jelly

Using this recipe you can dream up your own jellies using a variety of fruit juices. Try orange, blackcurrant, grape or passionfruit juice. Allow slightly more sugar when working with the more acid juices. Kiwi and pineapple juices are unsuitable since they contain an enzyme that stop the gelatine working.

1/4 litre (9 fl oz / 1 cup) mango juice
4 teaspoons black tea
3 egg yolks
80 g (3 oz / 1/3 cup) sugar
grated rind of one unsqueezed lemon
2 tablespoons lemon juice
2 cl (1 1/2 tablespoons) rum
2 envelopes (27 g / 1 oz) unflavoured gelatine
1/4 litre (9 fl oz / 1 cup) whipped cream
grated chocolate to garnish

Boil the mango juice and use it to make the tea. Allow it to stand for 4–5 minutes, then strain. Leave the tea to cool. Beat egg yolks with the cream until frothy. Add the lemon rind, juice and rum. Soften the gelatine with 4 tablespoons cold water for 10 minutes, then warm it gently over hot water, stirring constantly until it has completely dissolved. Gradually beat the gelatine into egg yolk mixture, then beat in the tea. As soon as the mixture begins to stiffen, fold in the whipped cream. Divide it between individual glasses and refrigerate. Serve garnished with grated chocolate.

Iced Passionfruit Tea

Passionfruit, is typical of Brazil where, like tea itself, it flourishes at a high altitude. The egg-shaped fruit measures 2–2 1/2 inches long and has a sweet-and-sour, aromatic flavour. Passionfruits vary in colour according to type and origin; they can be brownish, yellow or red. Passionfruit juice has a soothing effect and promotes sleep. Many passionfruit liqueurs are available, and passionfruit ice-cream has been popular for many years. Muesli with passionfruit syrup is a recommended breakfast treat. The Brazilians favour a rum punch containing rum, brandy, passionfruit juice and condensed milk, while the Peruvians go for a cocktail of brown and white rum, passionfruit juice and ice. The Hawaiians, on the other hand, are very fond of rum, passionfruit and orange juice, with dashes of Grand Marnier and angostura bitters for good measure.

3/4 litre (25 fl oz / 3 cups) water
10 teaspoons passionfruit tea
8 tablespoons pomegranate liqueur
125 g (5 oz / 1/2 cup) passionfruit
ice-cream

Bring the water to the boil and pour it over the tea; allow to brew for 4–5 minutes. Pour off tea and chill. Once chilled, mix it with the liqueur and divide up into individual glasses. Cut ice-cream into cubes and serve it with the drink.

Moroccan Tea

Broadly speaking, the range of North African drinks is as follows: water with meals, milk occasionally, the odd fruit juice with orange blossom water and wine that has to be exported because Muslims are unable to drink it. The same goes for Bouha, the Moroccan fig liqueur.

On the other hand, *thé la menthe* – mint tea – is served around the clock, in Tunisia as well as in Morocco. Even a guest who puts his head around the door for five minutes can expect to enjoy a refreshing glass. The recipe below is a somewhat simplified version of the rigmarole generally applied in Morocco, whereby the two types of tea are brewed separately, then blended by pouring from two pots simultaneously, like French *café au lait*.

1 peppermint tea-bag
1/4 litre (9 fl oz / 1 cup) water
4 teaspoons black tea
1/2 litre (18 fl oz / 2 cups) water
lump sugar

Brew the peppermint tea with 1/4 litre (9 fl oz) water and the black tea with 1/2 litre (18 fl oz). Leave for 4–5 minutes then strain. Mix the two together and sweeten with lump sugar before serving.

Mongolian Tea

The number and variety of recorded Mongolian tea recipes would certainly shake the preconceptions of the average European tea drinker. This recipe, for *mongolski chay*, is one of the least outrageous. The end product is similar to the kind of gruel served to patients with stomach complaints. As an example of other traditional types of tea, the Kalmuks prefer a brew consisting of green brick tea, fresh cream, butter and peppercorns.

1 tablespoon Assam tea
1/2 litre (18 fl oz / 2 cups) water
20g (3/4 oz / 1 1/2 tablespoons)
butter
30g (1 1/4 oz / 2 tablespoons) flour
1/8−1/4 litre (4−8 fl oz / 1/2−1 cup)
milk
40g (1 3/4 oz / 1/4 cup) boiled rice
a pinch of salt

Grind the tea finely with pestle and mortar, put in a pan and add water. Bring to the boil, then turn flame down to lowest setting. In another pan, heat all but 1 teaspoon of the butter, add the flour, and mix to a paste. Add milk gradually to this paste, stirring continually, and continue heating until the mixture reaches a creamy consistency. Add the rest of the butter and the rice. Turn this mixture out into the pan of tea, bring to the boil and add salt. Serve hot.

New Year's Cake

These are the traditional cakes that a Frisian household would offer to first footers, as well as sharing them out among the children. They would be washed down with Frisian tea, or maybe something a little stronger. You will need a griddle to cook them on.

250 g (9 oz / 1 cup) lump sugar
3/4 litre (26 fl oz / 3 cups) water
500 g (1 1/4 lbs / 4 cups) flour
1 small pinch salt
1 heaped teaspoon ground aniseed
1 teaspoon ground cinnamon
200 g (8 oz / 1 cup) butter
2 eggs

Dissolve the lump sugar in hot water. Sift the flour into a basin with the salt, aniseed and cinnamon. Melt the butter and mix to a dough with the eggs, sugar solution and flour. Spoon the dough onto a heated griddle and cook until crisp. As soon as each cake is done, quickly roll it round a wooden spoon, or fold over into a turnover. These rolls or turnovers can be filled with whipped cream.

Frisian Tea

It is customary in Friesland to keep a pot of tea ready at all times, just in case. Tea for breakfast is only the start of a typical Frisian tea-drinking day. Tea for "elevenses" is generally washed down with a measure of schnapps, and tea-time itself usually comes around between two and three in the afternoon. After dinner the pot can finally consider its day's work is done. The tea itself is a strong, dark brew – anything else is *Spölwater*, dishwater – sweetened with candied sugar and a *Wulkje Room*, a "cloud of cream" that must not be stirred.

The special Frisian tea blend can be obtained by post from Germany or from specialist shops.

1 litre (1 3/4 pints / 1 quart) water
6–7 heaped teaspoons Frisian tea
blend
4 sugar lumps
whipping cream if desired

Boil fresh water and brew up the tea in the pot; allow to stand for 3–4 minutes, then strain into a second pot. Drop a lump of sugar into each cup and fill to about the halfway mark with tea. Gently pour the cream over the back of a teaspoon into each cup but do not stir it. After the first cup, pour a second over the remaining sugar. There may even be enough left for a third cup too.

Old English Punch

Punch is a British discovery. According to the *Larousse Gastronomique*, the world's most comprehensive culinary reference work, punch was first prepared by British sailors in India in 1552. Even the name appears to have an Indian root; the word is derived from Hindi *puntscha* = five, because there are generally five main ingredients. The German poet, Schiller, was obviously not an initiate; his "Song of Punch", written in 1803, names only four ingredients, lemons, sugar, water and alcohol. "Swig it quick or it will give up the ghost", he wrote.

10 sugar cubes
1 untreated orange
1 untreated lemon
1 bottle red wine
3 tea cups strong black tea
4 cl (3 tablespoons) Curaçao

Place sugar in a pan with grated citrus rind and cook until yellow. Remove from the heat and slowly add a glass of red wine; stir until sugar mixture is dissolved. Now add the remaining wine and heat, but without allowing it to boil. Use a strong brew of tea (7–9 teaspoons to 1 litre [1 3/4 pints / 1 quart] of water), and blend with the wine while still hot. Add a dash of Curaçao and sweeten further if necessary.

Fiery Punch

This recipe is an adaptation of the traditional German *Feuerzangenbowle*, or German burning punch, mentioned elsewhere in the book, using white wine and tea. You will need all the equipment including the kettle (preferably of copper) the burner and loaf sugar, which can be bought in specialist shops, usually along with a bottle of rum. If you wish you can start warming the white wine before beginning to melt down the sugar loaf; that way the sugar dissolves more quickly. It is important to keep the wine below its boiling point however, as boiling drives off the alcohol.

1 litre (1 3/4 pints / 1 quart) strong tea
1 small sugar loaf (250 g / 10 oz)
1 small bottle high proof rum
2 bottles dry white wine
juice of one orange and one lemon

Prepare a strong brew of tea. Set up the punch kettle with the burner and loaf sugar; drench the sugar in rum (using a ladle, not direct from the bottle), ignite and wait until the sugar has completely melted into the kettle. Add rum continually throughout. Warm the white wine together with the tea and fruit juice, pour into the kettle and mix thoroughly with sugar and rum; serve piping hot.

French Apple Punch

This is an aromatic punch that derives its taste from apples and pineapple and is low in alcohol, thanks to a sparing contribution from the Calvados bottle. It is best drunk hot, but it may also be served cold in the summer. Calvados is a product of Normandy, where it was first recorded in 1553; it is distilled from cider whose production accounts for most of the annual harvest of nine billion apples.

For 4 to 6 servings:
1 litre (1 3/4 pints / 1 quart) strong tea
100 g (4 oz / 1/3 cup) brown lump or demerara sugar
500 g (1 1/4 lbs) cooking (sour) apples
1/2 fresh pineapple
1/2 lime
1/2 cinnamon stick
2 cloves
3 coriander seeds
3 allspice berries
1/8 litre (4 fl oz / 1/2 cup) Calvados
1/4 litre (9 fl oz / 1 cup) whipped cream
crushed brown lump sugar or demerara sugar to garnish

Prepare a strong brew of tea, pour it into a saucepan and add the sugar. Peel the fruit and slice it thinly. Add it to the tea with the spices. Bring to the boil and allow to stand for about 5 minutes over a low heat. Remove from the heat, add the Calvados and pass through a sieve directly into glasses. Top with whipped cream and sprinkle with the crushed sugar.

Japanese Tea Punch

There are not that many recipes using the kind of green tea preferred by the Japanese, but here is one of them. Green tea is available from good specialist shops, or by order. You will first have to accustom yourself to the flavour of this type of tea, since it contains a higher percentage of tannin than black tea. The fermentation process applied to black tea has a neutralizing effect. You might choose to strain off the tea after brewing, but you can also sweeten it and add lemon rind before doing so. A milder result can be obtained by using white rum (e.g. Bacardi) instead of Jamaican rum, or by reducing the overall alcohol content.

2 teaspoons Japanese green tea
1/2 litre (18 fl oz / 2 cups) water
250 g (9 oz / 1 cup) sugar
grated rind of one untreated lemon
2 bottles dry white wine
1 bottle Jamaica rum

Boil the water and allow to cool a little before brewing tea; leave the tea to stand for 4–5 minutes then strain off. Add sugar and lemon rind, and stir until sugar dissolves. Mix the wine and rum with the tea mixture and heat over a low flame without boiling. Serve from a bowl kept warm over a spirit burner.

Kirsch and Egg Punch

"The hard stuff" is often a good base for punch; aromatic rum, for example, or powerful arak, noble cognac or a good solid whisky. Warming kirsch should not be forgotten either, and this is the liquor used here. Anyone fooling around with these spirits should heed a few words of advice; your punch will stand or fall by the type and character of the drinks you use. It is better to drink punch or grog a little less often if you can guarantee an authentic result. Do not allow the final drink to boil away merrily before adding the tea, either. The more rapidly the water can be brought to the boil, the fresher the taste.

1 litre (1 3/4 pints / 1 quart) strong black tea
450 g (1 lb / 2 cups) granulated sugar
5 egg yolks
3/4 litre (26 fl oz / 3 cups) kirsch

Prepare a strong brew of tea and mix with a little over half the sugar while still hot. Beat the egg yolks with the remaining sugar and the kirsch until foaming. Continue beating as you add the mixture gradually to the tea, which should be kept over a low heat. Heat rapidly until the punch begins to foam, then serve.

Orange Punch

Do not be misled into thinking that for mixed drinks such as punch, it is possible to use ingredients that are not good enough to drink straight. The sort of temperature to which punch must be heated is guaranteed to highlight the weaknesses of your raw materials. The logic here is apparent when one remembers that a cheap wine or sparkling wine can be made to appear half-decent by serving it very cold; over the heat, the full aroma is released and even the strongest spices will not be able to conceal your misplaced thrift for long, so use first-class ingredients for punch!

3 untreated oranges
4 cl (3 tablespoons) rum
1/2 litre (18 fl oz / 2 cups) strong
black tea
250 g (9 oz / 1 cup) sugar
3 bottles of red wine
extra rum (optional)

Peel the oranges, slice thinly and remove pips. Drop the slices into a punch-bowl, sprinkle with sugar, cover in rum and allow to soak for about 2 hours. Prepare a strong brew of tea and mix with the remaining sugar. Add the red wine, then heat the whole mixture to just below boiling point and pour over the oranges. Add more rum for some extra pep if desired.

Planter's Punch

The classic planter's punch was a refreshing long drink made with lemon juice, light rum and assorted fruit. If the planter ever felt a little cold he preferred his punch warm, as detailed below.

To find out once and for all why rum is so called I pulled my reference books off the bookcase one by one. There was quite a heap by the time I reached the dictionaries on the bottom shelf. There, somewhere between "ruin" and "Rumania" I found the entry headed "rum". Did you know that Rum was the ancient name of *Konia* in Asia Minor, or that the Scottish island of Rum is part of the Inner Hebrides? Or that rum (the drink) is a corruption of the word "rumbullion" meaning "riot"?

1 litre (1 3/4 pints / 1 quart) strong black tea
200 g (7 oz / 2/3 cup) sugar
juice of three lemons
1/8 litre (4 fl oz / 1/2 cup) pineapple juice
1/2 bottle of Jamaica rum
2 cl (1 1/2 tablespoons) brandy

Prepare a strong brew of tea and dissolve the sugar in it. Add the fruit juice, then blend with the rum and brandy. Heat to just below boiling point before serving.

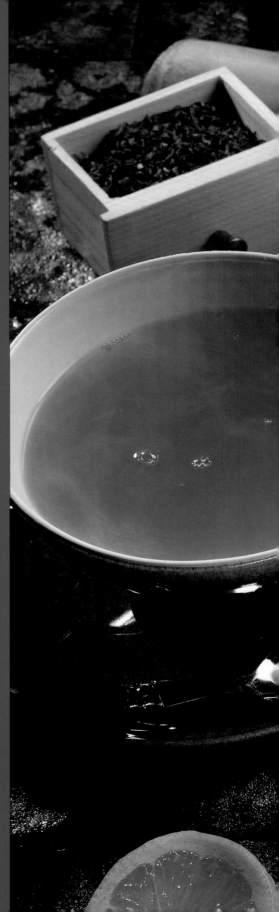

Punch Français

This recipe is for a French version of a punch which has a hint of the traditional German *Feuerzangenbowle*. According to the German writer Heinrich Spoerl, *Feuerzangenbowle* (a punch prepared with loaf sugar that melts and drips into a heated kettle of fortified wine) lies somewhere "between a drink in the accepted sense and sorcery. Beer affects the legs. Wine tickles the palate. Insidious spirits invade the brain. *Feuerzangenbowle*, however, determines your spiritual state. It wraps you up, defies gravity and envelopes everything in a fog."

3/4 litre (26 fl oz / 3 cups) hot black tea
500–750 g (1–1 1/2 lbs / 2–3 cups) granulated sugar
1 litre (1 3/4 pints / 1 quart) dark rum (54 %)
juice of 5 lemons and 5 oranges

Brew the tea in the usual way. Pour the rum over the sugar in a punch kettle and heat over a flame until sugar begins to turn brown. Add the tea and fruit juices. Reheat over a spirit burner before serving.

Royal Tea Punch

This "regal" punch is ideal for a children's summer party since it contains only fruit juice and no alcohol. Sugar can be added if necessary. The ice is not placed in the glasses themselves, but serves to cool the outside of the punch bowl. Some punch bowls have a glass container that can be filled with ice cubes and immersed in the bowl. Adding ice to the drink itself would give too watery a result, so if it is too strong, just add some extra soda water. Try the recipe with different juices depending on the season.

1/2 litre (18 fl oz / 2 cups) water
1 teaspoon black tea
1/4 litre (9 fl oz / 1 cup) grapefruit
juice
1/2 litre (18 fl oz / 2 cups) grape
juice
1/2 litre (18 fl oz / 2 cups) soda
water
ice cubes

Boil the water and brew tea for 4–5 minutes, strain off and chill. Combine the fruit juices with the tea and add soda water to thin. Serve from a punch bowl chilled on a bed of ice cubes.

Sloe Tea Punch

There is no need to wait for the first frost and brave the cold of the mountains to gather sloes for this punch. In an emergency you can always turn to the health food shop for bottled juice, and the same is true of sea buckthorn syrup. Sloes are members of the same family as plums and damsons, as can be deduced from their botanical name, *Prunus spinosa*. They grow everywhere from Siberia to central Europe; on the hill behind our house for instance, the stern limestone outcrops seem to be decked out in wedding dresses when the sloe-trees blossom. Sloes are recommended for stomach and kidney complaints, so this punch has a secondary medicinal purpose.

1 litre (1 3/4 pints / 1 quart) water
6 teaspoons black tea
1/2 litre (18 fl oz / 2 cups) sloe juice
1 1/2 tablespoons sea buckthorn syrup
100 g (4 oz / 1/2 cup) sugar
juice of one lemon

Boil the water, make the tea and allow it to brew for 3—4 minutes before straining it off. Mix the tea with the fruit juice, syrup and sugar in a pan. Heat to just below boiling point; serve in tea-glasses.

New Year's Eve Punch

The biggest punch-bowl of all time was a gift from Admiral Sir Edward Kennel to his men on October 25th, 1599. He ordered the drink to be prepared in a huge marble pool on his estate. The ingredients consisted of 80 kegs of spirits, 9 barrels filled with boiling water, 25,000 large lemons, 80 pints of lemon juice, 6 hundredweight of sugar, 5 pounds ground nutmeg, 300 biscuits (cookies) and a large barrel of Malaga wine. To protect this concoction against the elements, a canopy was erected over the pool of punch, which was served by a cabin boy who floated across the aromatic lake in a rosewood boat. A replacement was needed for the task every quarter of an hour since the alcoholic fumes soon took their toll. Whether you make it in a marble pool or in a more conventional punch-bowl, always use only the very best ingredients.

1 litre (1 3/4 pints / 1 quart) strong black tea
1 litre (1 3/4 pints / 1 quart) red wine
300 g (11 oz / 1 1/3 cups) sugar
1/2 litre (18 fl oz / 2 cups) arak

Brew the tea and heat it with the red wine, but do not allow it to boil before removing from the heat. Mix the sugar and arak, warming cautiously until the sugar is fully dissolved. Set light to the mixture and add it to the red wine and tea while still alight. Serve from a warmed punch bowl into heat-resistant pre-warmed glasses.

Tea Punch with Brown Candied Sugar

The Arabs candied sugar in the 9th century by letting a hot saturated sugar solution cool in huge glass jars. The sugar crystallized inside the jars but the jars had to be smashed to get at the crystals. A more economical method was later developed; wooden rods, reeds or lengths of wool were dipped into the sugar solution, around which the candy crystallized. Modern methods are more sophisticated. Brown candied sugar is hard to find but in the United States, you can use the Mexican version, *piloncillo*, and in Britain, use *jaggery*, obtainable at Indian grocers.

Rind of 1 untreated orange
juice of 2 lemons
1/2 bottle (0.375 litre / 13 fl oz)
brandy
1/2 litre (18 fl oz / 2 cups) water
4−5 teaspoons black tea
1 bottle red wine
100 g (4 oz / 1/2 cup) brown candied
sugar
2 cinnamon sticks
1/2 bottle rum
2 or 3 dashes of Campari

Grate the orange rind and combine it with the lemon juice and brandy; allow to soak for 2 hours and strain into a pan. Brew the tea using the water, then add to the pan along with the brown sugar candy and cinnamon sticks. Heat the mixture but do not boil. Finally add the rum and a couple of dashes of Campari. Serve hot.

Scotch Tea

It is said that anything considered fine by the Irish is despised by the Scots. Irish coffee, a blend of mocha, Irish whiskey, lump sugar and cream therefore has a counterpart in Scotch Tea, the creation of some ingenious Scottish tea-lovers, whose recipe can now be disclosed.

Whisky punches generally use Scotch, a blend of malt whisky and neutral grain spirit. Irish whiskey is not too bad, but Bourbon differs too much in flavour, and Canadian whisky gives it an unwanted twist. However, you could always experiment with your own favourite variations.

3/4 litre (25 fl oz / 3 cups) strong hot tea
4 sugar lumps
4 measures Scotch whisky
1/4 litre (8 fl oz / 1 cup) whipping cream
1 pinch grated nutmeg

Prepare a strong brew of tea, drop a sugar lump into each of the 4 earthenware mugs, cover with whisky and pour in the hot tea. Whip the cream and spice it with a pinch of nutmeg. Drink through the cool and soft cream topping.

Blackcurrant Tea Flip

Blackcurrants give this recipe its special character. Whereas redcurrants and whitecurrants are frequently eaten as fruit, blackcurrants tend to be converted into juice, syrups or liqueurs (such as Dijon Crème de Cassis, the popular French liqueur). Blackcurrants are acid, and rich in vitamin C, as well as providing B complex vitamins and a fair amount of tannin – up to 0.34 g per 100 g. Harvesting has been mechanized and the berries have been crossed and bred to make them easier for the machines to shake from the bushes.

1/2 litre (18 fl oz / 2 cups) water
7 teaspoons black tea
2 tablespoons dark brown sugar
1/4 litre (8 fl oz / 1 cup) blackcurrant juice
4 cl (3 tablespoons) white rum
4 cl (3 tablespoons) blackcurrant liqueur
1/8 litre (4 fl oz) whipped cream
grated chocolate to garnish

Boil the water and pour it over the tea and sugar. Allow to brew for 4–5 minutes, then strain off tea and chill. Add the rum, juice and liqueur to the cold tea, taste and adjust the flavour if necessary. Pour the drink into glasses, top each glass with whipped cream and garnish with grated chocolate.

Champagne Tea

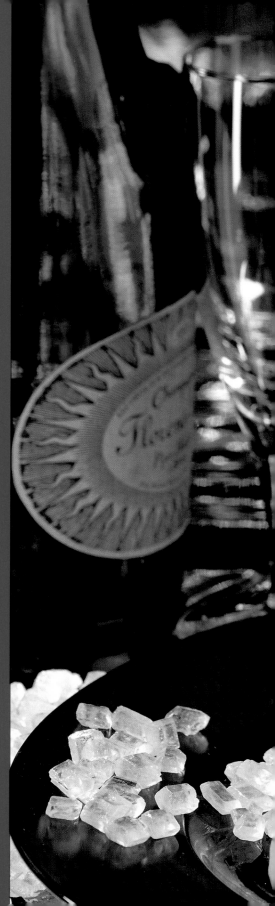

Though champagne appears in the name of this recipe, there is no reason why any other good quality sparkling wine should not be substituted. The only wines that may be called champagne are those from the Champagne region of France that have been manufactured to strict guidelines; German sparkling white wine, known as *Sekt*, is made with as much care and attention as its French half-brother and is a good substitute. The only point to watch is that the ingredients must be as cold as possible when mixed. This is best achieved by first filling the glasses with the chilled tea and then topping up with a bottle of wine fresh from the refrigerator.

1/4 litre (9 fl oz / 1 cup) water
4 teaspoons black tea
lump or granulated sugar if desired
juice of half a lemon
2 bottles of semi-dry champagne or
sparkling wine
4 slices of lemon

Boil the water, make the tea and allow it to brew for 4−5 minutes before straining it off and leaving to cool. Sweeten with sugar to taste, add lemon juice, then chill. Pour it into the glasses and top up with the chilled wine. Add a slice of lemon just before serving.

Tonic Tea

Tea made with milk instead of water makes a pleasant change. If you are making this tonic tea, be sure to use fresh milk and not UHT or tinned milk. Mixing with a whisk is the best way to ensure that your result turns out fresh and hot. Re-heating is not possible because of the egg content.

There is an eggnog recipe that is fairly similar to this one. Add 1/2 litre (18 fl oz / 2 cups) of whipping cream to a similar amount of strong tea and heat with sugar to taste. Whisk 4 egg yolks with 1/2 litre (18 fl oz / 2 cups) arak and add this mixture to the tea, stirring continuously – that's all.

3/4 litre (26 fl oz / 3 cups) milk
6 teaspoons black tea
3 egg yolks
1 tablespoon honey

Reserve a cupful of the milk. Heat the rest to just below boiling point and pour it over the tea. Allow the tea to brew for 3–4 minutes, then strain off. Beat the egg yolks and honey until creamy, then continue beating while adding the reserved milk. Finally add the tea mixture gradually, beating with a hand-held electric mixer for best results, and serve hot in glasses.

Tea Cream with Vanilla Ice

This unusual dessert would make a fitting end to an elaborate meal. The tea is used to flavour the whipped cream and provides an interesting counterpoint to the vanilla ice-cream. Arrange the cream decoratively using a spoon or a forcing bag for even greater effect. If you use gelatine to stiffen the cream, the dessert can be prepared well ahead of time and kept in the freezer. A very sweet ice cream will not need a great deal of extra sugar in the whipped cream – a little experimentation will point you down the right road. Serve with wafers or biscuits (cookies).

4 teaspoons black tea
1/4 litre (9 fl oz / 1 cup) whipping
cream
sugar to taste
12 scoops vanilla ice-cream
1 teaspoon ground cinnamon or
cocoa powder

Brew tea using only a couple of tablespoons of boiling water; strain off and chill the concentrate after letting it brew for 4–5 minutes. Whip the cream, adding sugar to taste and add the tea concentrate. Prepare 4 dishes of ice-cream, top with whipped cream and sprinkle with cinnamon or cocoa.

Tea Eggs

This is one of the few savoury recipes containing tea. *Cha yip dahn* is a Chinese hors d'oeuvre incorporating tea eggs. It is a highly decorative dish because the egg whites are patterned with a light brown tracery as a result of the cracking of the shells and are flavoured with a hint of cinnamon and aniseed. The original Chinese recipe calls for use of five-spice powder instead of the spices listed below. Soya eggs are another Chinese recipe, in which the eggs are shelled and boiled in a solution of dark soy sauce for half an hour, then served with a spicy sauce.

6 eggs
1 litre (1 3/4 pints / 1 quart) water
2 tablespoons black tea
1/4 cinnamon stick
1 star anise
2 tablespoons light soy sauce
salt
sugar

Hard boil the eggs then cool rapidly under the cold tap. Roll them under the palm of your hand on a hard surface until the shell is cracked all over, but do not remove them from the shell. Boil the water with the tea, cinnamon, star anise, soy sauce and a pinch of salt and sugar. Remove from the heat, add the eggs in their shells and simmer for half an hour over a very low heat until the shells turn brown. Leave the eggs to cool in the liquid and serve quartered or halved as a starter.

Tea Ice-cream

To ensure a good result from any ice-cream recipe in a household freezer, the mixture has to have the right fat content, provided in this case by the cream.

1/8 litre (4 fl oz / 1/2 cup) water
4 teaspoons black tea
1/2 litre (18 fl oz / 2 cups) whipping
cream
juice of three oranges
2 egg yolks
a little whipping cream to garnish
sugar to taste

Boil the water and brew the tea for about 3 minutes, then strain and chill. Use an electric mixer to combine the tea, whipping cream, orange juice and egg yolks thoroughly. Freeze in a tub, stirring occasionally during freezing. Serve in individual portions, garnished with a little sweetened whipped cream.

Tea Fizz

What is a real "fizz"? According to Peter Schmoeckel's standard barman's reference book, the fizz "... is the undisputed king of long drinks which tumbles down the throat like lemonade but sharpens both your wit and tongue". And he continues, "What do we get served as a fizz? Tired old dribs and drabs with just about enough energy to release the odd bubble, bitter offerings and lukewarm disasters". A fizz should be prepared in a shaker, and the tea fizz is no exception. Chill the glasses well beforehand and half fill them with crushed ice. Another tip is to use only freshly squeezed lemon juice rather than a commercial product. Finally, serve the drink immediately to avoid a bland, flat result.

Classic gin fizz is prepared with 2 bar spoons of cane syrup, the juice of one lemon, a measure of gin and soda water.

1/4 litre (9 fl oz / 1 cup) strong cold tea
2 tablespoons lemon juice
2 bar spoons maraschino liqueur
2 bar spoons granulated sugar or golden syrup
ice cubes

Chill a strong brew of tea and shake with the other ingredients in a cocktail shaker. Drop ice into a chilled glass and immediately pour the fizz over it.

Helsinki Tea

This is a refreshing summery recipe that retains the full flavour of the tea and has the advantage of being alcohol-free, making it ideal for children who enjoy the taste of tea. Most children's doctors are of the opinion that fairly weak tea is not dangerous for children. Just like adults, their ability to concentrate is increased by taking tea in small doses. Many prefer fruit teas such as strawberry or raspberry, and older ones enjoy making their own, too.

1/2 litre (18 fl oz / 2 cups) water
4—6 teaspoons tea
4 tablespoons sugar syrup made
50—100 g (2—4 oz / 1/4—1/2 cup)
sugar
1 apple
1 untreated lemon
4 fresh peppermint leaves

Boil the water and brew the tea for about 4 minutes before straining it off and leaving it to cool. Dissolve the sugar in 8 tablespoons boiling water and reduce to a thick syrup. Drop ice cubes into 4 cups or glasses and add 1 tablespoon of sugar syrup to each. Peel the apple and slice it thinly; place the slices over the ice. Top up with cold tea, and garnish with peppermint leaves and a slice of lemon.

English Tea-time Cake

On the Continent, this fruit cake is often simply called English cake. It is the perfect complement to afternoon tea or punch because of its moist, spicy texture. This is just one of the many speciality cakes often served with afternoon tea.

200 g (7 oz / 1 cup) butter
125 g (4 1/2 oz / 2/3 cup) sugar
1 pinch salt
grated rind of one untreated lemon
4 eggs
300 g (11 oz / 3 cups) self-raising flour
1 tablespoon rum
65 g (2 1/2 oz / 1/3 cup) candied lemon peel
65 g (2 1/2 oz / 1/3 cup) candied orange peel
100 g (4 oz / 1/2 cup) glacé cherries
200 g (7 oz / 3/4 cup) sultanas
100 g (4 oz / 1 cup) chopped almonds
butter for greasing tin (pan)
icing (confectioners') sugar for dusting

Cream the butter and mix in the sugar, salt, lemon rind and eggs thoroughly. Add the flour and rum and fold in the candied peel, coarsely chopped cherries, sultanas and almonds. Empty the mixture into a greased 30-cm (12-inch) loaf tin (pan) and bake in a preheated 350°F (175°C) oven for about 70–80 minutes. Turn out onto a wire rack when done and dust with the icing (confectioners') sugar.

Tea Liqueur

This is easy to prepare, preferably with green Japanese tea. No spices are listed below, but you might like to experiment by adding some. In Hochner's *Recipe Book of Practical Liqueur Manufacture* the recommended additives for "Fine Quality Essence of Tea" are lemon oil, orange blossom oil and rose oil or rose leaf extract, as well as Jamaica rum and arak for bouquet. You can take this any way you wish. Other old recipes advise use of vanilla, cinnamon, pineapple and sultana extracts. Use of grain spirit will save you effort, but you can also use 90% wine spirit, diluted to potable strength with distilled water.

100 g (4 oz / 1/2 cup) green Japanese tea leaves
1/4 litre (9 fl oz / 1 cup) water
3 litres (5 1/4 pints / 3 quarts) grain spirit
sugar syrup made with 350 g (14 oz / 2 cups) sugar to 2 litres (3 1/2 pints / 2 quarts) water

Brew the tea for 4–5 minutes and add it with the leaves to the grain spirit. Allow to stand overnight then strain, mix with sugar syrup and rack off. Leave for a few days before beginning to sample.

Tea Parfait

No prizes for guessing that the parfait originated in France. It is usually prepared with
the finest ingredients. The best-known
savoury versions are made from goose-liver
and lobster. Ice-cream and cinnamon parfaits
are also popular; this tea parfait uses cream
rather than gelatine to give it body. You will
find the result is easier to serve if the egg-yolk-
and-tea mixture is warmed to a thick cream in
a bain-marie. Whipped cream can then be
folded in once the mixture has cooled slightly.
Once it has set in the fridge or freezer, it will
turn out easily. It is up to you to choose the
type and size of dish that you use as a mould
for the parfait.

1/8 litre (4 fl oz / 1/2 cup) water
3 tablespoons black tea-leaves
4 egg yolks
125 g (4 1/2 oz / 2/3 cup) sugar
2 teaspoons lemon juice
8 tablespoons passionfruit juice
1/4 litre (9 fl oz / 1 cup) whipping
cream

Boil the water and brew the tea for 4–5
minutes; strain it and leave to cool. Beat the
egg yolks and sugar until foaming then add
the cold tea and juices. Fold in the whipped
cream and divide the parfait into individual
moulds which should then be chilled for
40–50 minutes in the freezer compartment.

Toddy

Toddy is a traditional British hot drink. Whisky is often used, but as here, rum also makes an excellent basis; the main thing is to serve it hot. There is a similar whisky recipe known as "Old Man's Milk" which uses 4 egg yolks beaten with 4 tablespoons of sugar. This is then mixed with 1/2 litre (18 fl oz / 2 cups) of milk. The final ingredient is a whole bottle of whisky and a light dusting of nutmeg to round it off.

While on the subject of whisky, there was some dismay at a Canadian computer company recently when tests were run on a new computer translation system. Faced with the problem of translating the Bible text "The spirit is willing but the flesh weak" the computer came up with "Whisky is recommended but meat is not so good".

For one person:
1/8 litre (4 fl oz / 1/2 cup) hot black tea
2 sugar cubes
1 piece of cinnamon
2 cloves
1 piece of lemon rind
Jamaica rum

Prepare the tea. Drop sugar cubes into a warmed mug and fill it about 2/3 full of tea; top up with rum and enjoy immediately.

Profiteroles with Tea Cream

Choux pastry requires a little skill.

For the batter:
1/4 litre (9 fl oz / 1 cup) water
125 g (4 1/2 oz / 1/2 cup) butter
125 g (4 1/2 oz / 1 cup) plain flour
3–4 eggs
For the filling:
1/2 litre (18 fl oz / 2 cups) milk
200 g (7 oz / 3/4 cup) sugar
3 teaspoons black tea
1 sachet custard powder
4 egg yolks
200 g (7 oz / 3/4 cup) butter
1 pinch salt
icing sugar (confectioner's sugar)

For the batter: Boil the water with the butter. Add all the flour at once, and beat with a wooden spoon until the batter reaches a smooth consistency. Heat for about 1 minute stirring continuously. It should form into a lump, which must be allowed to cool slightly. Turn the mixture out into a basin and beat in the eggs until the mixture becomes shiny and stands up in stiff peaks. Place teaspoonfuls of the mixture on a baking sheet (tray) lined with greaseproof paper and bake for 20–30 minutes in a pre-heated 420–450°F (200–220°C) oven. Split the profiteroles as soon as they come out of the oven.

For the filling: Heat the sugar with 2/3 of the milk and pour this over the tea-leaves; leave to brew for 4–5 minutes then strain off. Whisk the remaining milk with the custard powder and egg yolks. Re-heat the milk to just below boiling point, remove it from heat and stir in the custard mixture. Bring to the boil rapidly, stirring constantly, then leave to cool. Combine butter and salt and mix gradually into the custard. Spoon the cream into the profiteroles and dust them with sifted icing sugar.

Glossary of teas and related terms, from A for Africa to Y for Yunnan-Darjeeling

Africa: The majority of the tea plantations in African countries were set up on the initiative of the British colonial power. At first, tea was mass-produced to the English taste and then blended. Garden teas are found only in Kenya on the highland plantations. Other tea-growing countries include Burundi, Cameroon, Malawi, Mozambique, Zimbabwe, Rwanda, Tanzania and Uganda.

Afternoon: A traditional British tea blend for the afternoon, consisting of Ceylon and Assam teas of the Flowery Orange Pekoe grade. Afternoon teas have a lighter flavour and colour than the strong breakfast teas.

Anamalai: A tea region in the south of India, in the area of mountains and plateaus of Anamalai ("Elephant Mountain") which is within the Madras administrative district. These teas are strong and rich in tannin, and are mainly used in blends. The strongest flavours are obtained by picking during the monsoon, in spring and summer, while more aromatic teas are picked mainly in autumn and winter.

Anhui: This Chinese province in the lower reaches of the Chang Jiang river (Yangtze Kiang), formerly written Anhwei, encompasses the Keemun tea area.

Argentina: A young tea-growing country which produces standard tea using modern methods. This tea is used in blends for export.

Aromatic tea: Tea scented with fresh blossoms or essences has been produced in China for over 2000 years. The blossoms of jasmine, roses, magnolias, hibiscus or lychees are added during processing. On the other hand, essences, essential oils or other aromatic substances may be added to the finished tea. Oil of bergamot (Earl Grey tea), vanilla, bitter orange, citrus fruits, ginger, lavender or mint are among those used. Both green and black teas can be scented.

Assam: This tea district, which extends along both sides of the Brahmaputra River in northern India, is the largest tea-growing area in the world. Assam tea is generally strong and fragrant and blends well with lighter types from the younger tea-growing countries. Assam tea is a major constituent of traditional English and Frisian blends. The first tea-gardens were established in Assam by British planters in 1832. Nowadays, Assam accounts for some half of all Indian tea production and 15 per cent of the world production.

Assam plants: Tea shrubs of the genus *Camellia assamica*, originating from the bushes which grew in the wild in Assam. Assam plants are more productive and less delicate than the China tea plants, but do not have as fine an aroma.

Auctions: In most tea-producing countries auctions take place at regular intervals. They are held in Calcutta for northern India, in Cochin for southern India, in Colombo for Ceylon/Sri Lanka, in Djakarta for Indonesia and in Nairobi for East Africa. European auctions are held in Amsterdam, Antwerp and London.

Autumnal: Assam and Darjeeling teas harvested between the summer monsoon and the onset of winter. Teas picked at this time are generally low in tannin content and have a fine aroma, especially when the autumn has been sunny.

Bakey: Describes a tea that has been fired at too high a temperature, giving it an undesirable "burnt" aroma.

Bancha: A Japanese green tea for everyday use, competing in the same market as cheap teas from China and Taiwan. The same plant provides Gyokuro in spring and Sencha in autumn, as well as Bancha in summer.

Bangladesh: The tea varieties grown in Bangladesh are similar to those grown in neighbouring India and are only exported in small quantities, mostly to Pakistan. English and Frisian blends often contain tea from Bangladesh.

Bannockburn: A plantation laid out to the north of Darjeeling in about 1860. It produces mainly high quality Chinese varieties in small quantities.

Basket-fired: Japanese tea fired in baskets over an open flame.

Bhutan: This independent state in the Himalayas to the east of Darjeeling supplies small quantities of tea of below average quality, most of which is for home consumption.

Black tea: Fermented tea whose leaves turn red during fermentation, then black during drying. It is the preferred choice in most countries of the world.

Blends: Tea from a particular region tastes different every year according to the prevailing weather conditions. Since many consumers like to be able to identify a certain taste, merchants compensate by mixing the teas to conform to a certain standard. The tea-taster's job is to identify the types of tea that complement each other in this way. Russian, Frisian and English are examples of well-known blends. These blends can also be adjusted to local conditions, such as hardness of water.

Body: The aroma and colour of a tea.

Bohea: Former general description for all black China teas, derived from the name of a certain Chinese growing region. It was Bohea tea which was tipped into the harbour during the Boston Tea Party.

Bold: Trade term for a tea whose leaves are too coarse and must be put through the mill again.

Brazil: Tea has been grown in Brazil for over 100 years, largely by Japanese growers. The chief product is BOP bulk tea and fannings for the home market and international bulk dealers.

Bread-and-Butter teas: Run-of-the-mill teas without any particular qualities. They are usually the result of being picked during the rainy season.

Breakfast: Traditional English blend of Ceylon BOP and smaller amounts of Assam BOP or Darjeeling BOP. They tend to produce a very strong infusion.

Brick Tea: Green China tea, usually the smallest grades (fannings, dust) and of low quality, pressed into hard bricks or bars. It was developed for ease of transport, allowing camels to be loaded more economically. Of little significance today, but very decorative, as it is pressed into patterned moulds.

Bright: Strong, luminous, red infusion.

Brisk: A refreshing, lively tea (as opposed to a flat tea).

Broken: Teas whose leaves are reduced in size by rolling or cutting. These teas give a higher yield than leaf tea; the greater part of modern tea production belongs in this category.

Broken Orange Pekoe (BOP): The main variety of broken tea.

Broken Orange Pekoe Fannings (BOPF): The third smallest grading in India, used mainly for tea-bags.

Brunch Tea: Current English tea blend for Sunday brunch. A large-leafed blend, chiefly of Darjeeling and Assam.

Cachar: A north Indian tea district, situated between Bangladesh and the Burmese border. The first plantations were set up well before 1860. Nowadays, strong tea varieties of medium quality are produced.

Caddy: A container for the storage of tea, once in common use, but today a sought-after collector's item. Caddies are generally fitted with separate containers for green and black tea and provided with a spoon and a bowl to mix one's own blend. The British housewife kept the key to the caddy on her key-ring to prevent her staff being tempted to remove some of the expensive tea.

Calcutta: Long-established centre of the international tea trade.

Camellia: The botanical name for the genus to which the tea shrub belongs. A distinction is made between *Camellia assamica* from Assam and *Camellia sinensis* from China. The tea hybrids widely found nowadays are cultivated from these two species.

Caravan tea: China tea that came overland by beast of burden to Russia before the completion of the Suez Canal (1869) cut the sea voyage from central Asia. Tea that came overland was more highly sought after than that which had to endure a long sea voyage in the damp hold of a sailing vessel; caravan tea was consequently more expensive. Russia was a staging post through which much of the caravan tea passed on its way to Europe.

Castleton: A fairly small but nevertheless highly regarded plantation in the south of Darjeeling, largely given over to growing China teas. The second flush from this garden produces some of the world's very best teas.

Celadon ware: Traditional porcelain from China, Korea and Japan first used around the year 1000 AD. In China the green jade-like glaze is known as Quing.

Ceylon: The world's second largest tea producer after China and India. Despite the recent adoption of a new name, Sri Lanka, the teas retain the name Ceylon. The island's chief product around the turn of the 19th century was coffee. In 1870, all the island's coffee plantations fell victim to a fungus disease and a plague of rats. The planters then switched to growing Chinese cinnamon (cassia) which caused a slump in world prices. Even Ceylon's other traditional crop, cinnamon, could not make up the deficits that started to be incurred, so intensive planting of tea came to the rescue. Most Ceylon teas are full-flavoured and have a good colour. Uva in the east of the island, Dimbula in the west and Nuwara Eliya in the central highlands are the most important growing regions; all of them lie between 1,000 and 7,000 feet above sea level.

Chabako: Chest for storing tea used in the Japanese tea ceremony.

Chadô: According to Zen Buddhism, "the way of tea".

Cha-hiki-usu: Hand-powered tea mill, once in widespread use in Japan for pulverizing green tea.

Chainik: Russian word for a teapot.

Chaire: Japanese lacquered wooden, bamboo or earthenware box for storing tea. Chaires fetch high prices among collectors.

Chanoyu: The Japanese tea ceremony.

Chanoyu kaiseki: A combination of the Japanese tea ceremony and a meal, a Japanese tea-party.

Chasen: Japanese bamboo tea-whisk shaped like a shaving brush and used for beating brewed tea until frothy. The chasen is kept in a special bamboo sheath, the chasenzutsu.

Chawan: Ceramic Japanese tea-bowl without handles. It is the focal point of the tea ceremony. The traditional shape fits snugly into the hand, and invites the use of the second hand too. The material of which the bowl is made varies according to the rank of ceremony being performed. It is generally plain but can also be elaborately decorated.

Chest: The plywood tea-chest, with tin-reinforced corners and lining of tissue paper and foil is a familiar sight to anyone who has moved house. A chest contains 40 to 50 kilograms (88 to 110 lbs) of tea.

China: The home of tea and tea cultivation. Tea was known in China 5000 years ago, and has been cultivated for over 3000 years. China is second only to India as a producer of tea, but because of the vast home market, exports less than both India and Sri Lanka. Green tea is most popular in China but black tea is also produced, as is Oolong, a semi-fermented tea. China tea is famous for its fine aroma. The Chinese themselves tend to drink tea without either sugar or milk, and therefore prefer aromatic teas.

China plants: Shrubs of the species *Camellia sinensis*, the original Chinese tea plant.

China Caravan: A traditional Chinese blend, so-called because it was once transported by caravan from China to Russia and Tibet. This tea is generally mild and aromatic with a full-bodied flavour.

China White Tips: Traditional Chinese blend of leaves with white tips, usually Lapsang or Tarry Souchong with small amounts of unsmoked green teas. Notable for its light infusion, aroma and slightly smoky flavour.

Ching wo: Low quality China tea from Fuzhou (Fuchow) in southern China.

Chittagong: Tea-growing region and port in Bangladesh.

Chop: The expression used in the trade for the tea harvest. The first crop of the year is termed the first chop.

Chung Hao: High-quality green China tea, scented with Jasmine blossom, also known as "Emperor's Tea". It is rarely exported, and even then only in small quantities.

Chun mee: Green Chinese tea with slightly bitter flavour.

Cinnamon Tea: Black tea scented with cinnamon from Madagascar.

Cisaruni: Black Java tea, renowned for its fruitiness and perkiness.

Clean: Term used to refer to a tea with a pure, neutral aroma, or a blend free of fannings or dust.

Cochin: Centre for tea trade, auctions and export in southern India. Most aromatic Cochin teas are blended.

Cold weather tea: Tea harvested in Assam, Sri Lanka and southern India during the winter months; dry, cool weather causes slow growth, resulting in a highly aromatic product. Because the harvest tends to be small it is also a fairly expensive type of tea.

Colour: The colour of a brew is no sign of its quality, neither does it give any indication of its content. It has much to do with the size of the leaf particles; dust and fannings thus colour more quickly than leaf or broken teas whose particles are larger. Colour also depends on the degree of oxidization that occurs during fermentation. Green tea exported from China used to be coloured artificially using Prussian blue and gypsum, a practice now forbidden.

Congou: Black China tea producing a light but aromatic brew.

Country Greens: Chinese green tea producing a brew that shimmers green and gold.

Creamy: Description of a tea on whose surface a milky skin forms after cooling, produced by a combination of caffeine and casein. In the case of good Assam teas, it is seen as a sign of high quality.

CTC tea: A modern tea production process that makes heavy use of machinery. Tea-leaves are first torn up by toothed rollers before final rolling. This has the effect of breaking down the cell structure more than previous methods, causing greater oxidization during fermentation, and making the tea more productive. CTC teas only occur among broken teas. The abbreviation stands for crushing, tearing, curling.

Cup: Term used by tea-tasters for the infusion used for tasting, after the leaves have been strained out.

Cutter: Machine for turning the raw leaf tea into a broken product.

Darjeeling: Tea-growing region in the Himalayas of northern India, at an altitude of 3,000 to 7,200 feet. Its monsoon climate is responsible for the very flowery varieties that grow here, some of which are the very best available anywhere. Tea has been grown there since 1834. Although Darjeeling was best known as a resort for officers and officials of the British Raj, some of the first tea planters in the area were German missionaries. Darjeeling is used in many tried and trusted blends, but is also often sold as a garden tea.

Dead tea: Murky, poor quality infusion.

Deshima: Portuguese and later Dutch trading port in Japan (Nagasaki).

Dickoya: Sri Lankan tea district near Dimbula and with a similar output.

Dimbula: Region of western Sri Lanka whose first tea-gardens were established before 1870. Its teas, especially those harvested during the dry season, are aromatic, dry and full.

Dooars: A region between Darjeeling and Assam in India that produces excellent teas, most of which are sold blended with the products of its better known neighbours.

Dull: An infusion lacking clarity and luminosity is described as dull. The term is also used by the trade to describe flavour.

Dust (D): Smallest, and very strong type of tea, with high tannin content. Often used in tea-bags.

Earl Grey: Black tea scented with oil, extracted from the rind of the bergamot orange, a bitter citrus fruit. Edward Grey, Earl of Falloden, the British Foreign Secretary, came across an ancient Chinese recipe during his travels and on his return passed it on to a London firm who expressed their thanks by naming it after the Earl. Today, every tea manufacturer in the world lists Earl Grey in their range.

Early Morning Tea: The first "cuppa", drunk by an Englishman as soon as he rises. Hotel guests in the British Isles and elsewhere in the Empire could once count on being woken up with a fresh brew of tea. Today this tends to be the exception rather than the rule.

Earthy: Describes an unpleasant taste that is usually caused by storage of tea in damp conditions.

English Blend: Traditional blend to cater for the English palate, originally composed of Ceylon, Indian and China teas, but lately tending to comprise economical varieties from up-and-coming tea-growing countries such as Kenya, Tanzania, Malawi and Mozambique. A standard English blend must be cheap and develop a full flavour rapidly. Tea is usually drunk with milk in England, and often with sugar too.

Enza: A plump, round cushion covered in loosely woven fabric used by guests at the tea ceremony in Japan who wish to sit European style.

Estates: Sri Lankan tea plantations.

Fannings: The second smallest size of uncut tea, larger only than dust. Fannings are usually used in tea-bags and produce a strong infusion that colours rapidly.

Fermentation: Tea-manufacturing process which, strictly speaking, has nothing to do with fermentation, being a process of oxidization. Only black tea is fermented; Chinese Oolong is semi-fermented, while green tea escapes the process altogether.

Fibrous: Containing a lot of wood fibres. Applies particularly to fannings and dust.

Fine Tippy Golden Flowery Orange Pekoe 1 (FTGFOP 1): The finest quality tea according to the Indian scale, with high tip content.

Firing: The drying process after fermentation.

First flush: The first crop in northern India after the spring monsoon. Only the delicate pale-green tips are picked, which produce a very flowery and lively brew. Teas from the first crop are highly prized, so much so that they are often airfreighted to Europe.

Five o'clock tea: The late afternoon tea-break, when light aromatic teas are usually served.

Flavour: In the tea trade, flavour refers to the aroma of a tea; the term is often applied to highland teas.

Flakey: Carelessly manufactured tea with flat, badly wrinkled or rolled leaves.

Flowery: High quality teas picked just as the youngest leaves have begun to develop.

Flowery Broken Orange Pekoe (FBOP): Term in use in India for a good quality broken tea.

Flowery Orange Pekoe (FOP): Outdated British term for the coarse product of a harvest that gives a light, thin brew.

Fluff: Unpleasant dust affecting black tea-leaves which becomes very apparent during blending and sieving.

Flush: The youngest two leaves and a bud on the tea-bush, picked during harvesting. First flush = first crop. Second flush = the later harvest that year.

Frisian blend: Although the Frisians account for only 4 per cent of the population of the Federal Republic of Germany, they consume about 25 per cent of the country's tea imports. Frisian blend tends to consist of Assam teas bulked with African varieties. The Frisians' taste for tea has historical roots, having been acquired from their Dutch neighbours. Frisian blend is usually brewed very strong and drunk with candied sugar and fresh cream, traditionally three cups at a time.

Fujian: Province in southern China formerly known in Europe as Fukien. It is a traditional tea-growing region whose mountains support a type of tea with a particular flavour and taste. Fujian teas are exported from the nearby ancient port of Fuzhou (Foochow).

Furo: Charcoal stove for heating water used in the Japanese tea ceremony. Glowing embers are contained in a bronze, iron or ceramic pot on a bed of ashes. The furo is for use in summer only; in winter it is replaced by the ro.

Fuzhou (Foochow): The export port serving the southern Chinese province of Fujian. The famous tea-clippers departed from here after the Opium Wars.

Garden teas: Varieties of tea from particular plantations, sold with proof of their origin.

Gielle: Highly regarded plantation in the east of the Darjeeling region producing quality leaf teas, mainly from China plants.

Ginger tea: The best ginger teas are scented with pieces of dried root ginger.

Golden: Term used to describe tea containing light tips with low tannin content.

Golden Broken Orange Pekoe (GBOP): Indian term for a high quality broken tea.

Golden Flowery Orange Pekoe (GFOP): Indian term for the third best quality tea.

Gon Jim (silver needle): Green China tea from the province of Guangdong (Kwangtung), served during meals to refresh the gums between courses. Also known as Ngun Jum.

Grades: The dried leaves are passed over sieves and sorted by size. The descriptive terms are thus applied to sizes rather than quality (see under "leaf grades").

Grof: Dutch word for "coarse", applied to Broken Orange Pekoe for instance. Commonly used in Indonesia as a relic of the colonial past.

Green tea: Unfermented tea, formerly widespread, but now the most popular form of tea only in China, Japan and Taiwan. The crop is subjected to very high temperatures to kill off enzymes, but the green of the leaf is retained. Green tea tends to be drier than black, and only develops its full aroma when brewed with soft water. It is best to brew it with water at a temperature of 60 °C to 85 °C, boiled rapidly then allowed to cool.

Guangxi (Kwangsi): Province in southern China on the Gulf of Tonkin.

Gunpowder: Chinese green tea whose leaves are rolled into balls. British merchants were responsible for the name. It produces a mild, pale infusion.

Gyokuro: High quality Japanese green tea from the Shizuoka region on the slopes of Fujiyama. The first crop of gyokuro produces excellent teas generally reserved for special occasions.

Hakobidate: The simplest form of Japanese tea ceremony. Rather than being served in front of guests on tables, the paraphernalia is brought in ready for service, and carried out at the end.

Harsh: Harshness tends to be caused by using unripe leaves picked when too large.

Hassun: Small rectangular wooden tray of cedar or kiri used during the Japanese tea ceremony.

Heavy: A heavy tea is usually the result of over-fermentation; the term is applied to a thick, not very fresh brew.

Hibachi: Type of grill (broiler) used during the Japanese tea ceremony, fired with charcoal for heating water.

Highgrown: Ceylon tea grown over 4,000 feet above sea level.

Highland: Generic term for the highland regions of Sri Lanka which produce the island's finest and most aromatic teas (Dickoya, Dimbula, Nuwara Eliya and Uva).

High range: Tea-growing region of southern India producing better-than-average black teas.

High tea: A meal in itself in British culture when tea is served as an accompaniment to cakes, sandwiches and biscuits in the south, and a substantial cooked meal in the north.

Hishaku: Japanese bamboo ladle used to transfer water from the kettle into bowls. Sometimes also made of cedar or cypress.

Hoochows: Chinese black tea producing a light, thin infusion often incorporated into simple blends.

Hung pien (chrysanthemum): Black tea from China's Zhejiang (Chekiang) province, containing dried chrysanthemum leaves. Drunk with Chinese cakes and often sweetened with sugar.

Hybrids: Bushes bred by crossing China and Assam plants, the basis of most of the world's cultivated teas. Hybrids are designed to produce a good, high quality crop and to be resistant to pests and disease.

Hyson: Chinese green tea variety from the Singlo mountain area of Kingnan. Chinese tradition has it that the very first tea was harvested here. The name comes from the characters denoting "hee" and "chun" used by a certain tea merchant as his trademark. Today, green teas produced elsewhere are also called hyson.

Ihsing-Ton: Fireproof china produced in the Chinese city of the same name. The tea-making utensils, some unglazed others highly colourful, have been famous for hundreds of years and show no signs of losing their popularity.

Illam: Nepalese tea variety with a delicate flowery character.

Imperial: Coarse Chinese green tea rejected during manufacture of gunpowder tea.

Imperial Or: Modern Chinese blend of lightly smoked black tea, to which small quantities of jasmine tea are added.

India: The world's largest tea producer supplying mainly black teas, but also green varieties in small quantities. The most important districts in the north are Assam, Cachar, Darjeeling, Dooars and Terai; in the south, they are Nilgiri, Anamalai and Cochin. Annual exports amount to about 200,000 tonnes.

Indonesia: Tea-growing here is largely confined to the islands of Java and Sumatra whose strong, dry crops are preferred for blending. The harvesting takes place all year round. The United States, Pakistan and Egypt are the largest importers of Indonesian tea.

Iran: Tea production in Iran, centered in the north of the country, is so insignificant that it is unable even to satisfy domestic demand. Iranian tea is therefore only rarely found on the international commodity markets.

Japan: Tea cultivation was brought to Japan by Buddhist monks between the 6th and the 8th centuries. Most of the crop, both of black and of green teas, is sold on the home market, which relies on imports to keep up with demand. The tea ceremony, though once of religious significance, is nowadays more of a social occasion.

Jasmine tea: A very common green or Oolong tea from the Fuzhou (Foochow) region scented with jasmine blossom.

Jungpana: Tea garden in the Darjeeling district, producing teas with a nutmeg-like aroma.

Kakemono: A scroll decorated with a brushwork illustration or Japanese characters, hung in an alcove of the room during the Japanese tea ceremony. Lucky themes are preferred, in accordance with the spirit of the ceremony itself.

Kama: Kettle made of cast-iron or bronze, used in the Japanese tea ceremony to heat the water for the tea. Japanese reference books list over fifty different types of kama. The woven mat on which the kettle is placed is called a kamashiki.

Kayu-Aro: The largest tea plantation in the world, on the Indonesian island of Sumatra. It has an area of about 5,560 acres which yields 4,500 tonnes of tea annually.

Keemun: Famous tea-growing district of China whose teas are particularly prized around the world for their aroma, smoothness and delicacy. In England Keemun is regarded as the ideal breakfast tea. The Chinese imperial court also preferred the fine Keemun varieties. Keemun is particularly recommended for tea-drinkers with sensitive stomachs, since its tannin and caffeine content are low.

Kenya: This leading country among the young African tea countries produces strong bulk teas for blends but also aromatic garden teas. Most of the plantations lie in the vicinity of the town of Kericho at an ideal altitude. Kericho has its own Tea Hotel which is the starting point for sightseeing tours of the plantations. The port for exporting Kenyan tea is Kilindini, the newly built harbour of Mombasa, which is also the largest port on the east African coast.

Kintuk: Black tea variety from China and Taiwan.

Kueihua: Semi-fermented China tea (Oolong), scented with the blossoms of Chinese cinnamon (Cassia).

Lapsang Souchong (Su tang): Large-leafed black China tea from Hunan and Fujian. Hearty and full, with a strong, smoky flavour.

Lavender tea: A popular black tea drunk in France, and scented with dried lavender blossoms or lavender oil.

Lay Jee (Lychee): Black tea or Oolong, scented with yellow lychee blossoms, chiefly from Taiwan. It is particularly popular among the Cantonese who believe it has the power to renew old friendships.

Leaf grade (see also "Leaf tea"): Abbreviations and their meanings are explained in detail in the introduction.

Leaf tea: Includes the largest grades FTGFOP 1, FTGFOP and GFOP (on the Indian scale) and FOP, OP, P and PS (the old British scale). Leaf teas can be left to brew for slightly longer than broken teas.

Light: Used to describe a tea whose liquor remains very pale, but which can nevertheless have an aromatic fragrance and a fresh flavour.

Lingia: Indian tea-garden in western Darjeeling, near the Nepalese border, with valuable but small scale production.

Lok-on tea: Black China tea from Yunnan province, sold in compressed form in bamboo baskets. It is said to promote good digestion and slimming.

Lord's Tea: Traditional blend of Ceylon and Assam teas, producing a strong dark liquor.

Lotus tea: Black China tea scented with lotus blossoms.

Low grown: Ceylon tea from tea-gardens on the lower slopes (up to about 2,000 feet), lighter and less aromatic than teas grown at higher altitutdes.

Lu An (Clear Distance): Strong black China tea from the Guangdong province. It is best served at mealtimes and late at night.

Lung Chin (Dragon Well): Green China tea from the Hangzhou province, regarded as the finest green tea. Light, fresh in colour and lightly perfumed, it has a mild and gentle nature. Suitable for drinking day and night.

Lung So (Dragon's Beard): Green tea from the Chinese province of Guangdong, with a light colour and a delicate aroma. An afternoon tea for social occasions.

Lu Shan Wu: A traditional green China tea from the mountainous region of Nanning in the Guangxi (Kwangsi) province. The best varieties grow below the frequently overcast mountain peaks.

Makaibari: Indian tea-garden to the south of Darjeeling, mainly planted with hybrids.

Malabar: Renowned tea-garden on the Indonesian island of Java.

Malawi: This young African tea country mainly produces bulk, Ceylon-type teas. The first plantations were laid out at the turn of the century.

Malaysia: Small plantations laid out by the Chinese which produce light and cheap bulk tea, which lends itself to blends. The tea is harvested all year round. The best of the crop is consumed locally.

Malty: A malty flavour is prized by tea connoisseurs.

Maracuja tea: Black tea scented with the passionfruit, imported into Britain and the United States from continental Europe.

Matcha: Japanese pulverized green tea which is also used for the tea ceremony.

Mat (botanical name, Ilex paraguayensis, also known as Paraguay tea, Jesuit tea or yerba-maté): A herbal tea with various properties which include suppressing the appetite, calming the nerves and promoting sleep. It is produced from the dried leaves of a South American variety of holly and is a popular beverage in South America. When freshly prepared, it has an exquisite, lightly smoky aroma.

Midgrown: Ceylon tea grown at medium altitude (2,000 to 4,000 feet).

Montmartre: A black tea popular in France, with a fragrance of green apples and a hint of aniseed.

Mook Lay Far: Black or Oolong tea, usually from Taiwan, scented with fresh or dried jasmine blossoms. This fragrant, pale-yellow tea is often taken in the afternoon or between meals, and is also suitable for drinking with heavy meals.

Mudis: Tea-growing district around the town of Mudis in the Anamalai region of southern India. The plantations produce a crop of good quality strong teas.

Musty: Mustiness is caused at source by packing tea that has not been properly dried.

Nepal: Tea-growing on the slopes of the Himalayas has been promoted by the Nepalese government; most of the crop is in the form of mildly aromatic black teas, chiefly for home consumption.

Neutral: A brew with no striking characteristics.

New Guinea: Commercial tea-growing is a recent development here, and some of the country's broken highland teas produce very interesting brews.

Night Shadow: Japanese green tea from the Shizuoka region not far from Fujiyama.

Nilgiri: Leading region of southern Indian tea production, with gardens situated up to an altitude of 6,000 feet, producing a year-round crop. Nilgiri tea tends to have a fine but intense aroma. Good weather teas from Nilgiri are highly prized.

Nonsuch: Highly regarded tea garden in the Nilgiri Mountains north of Cochin. Nonsuch teas produce a delicate infusion with a pronounced aroma.

Nutty: Second flush teas from the dry season in Sri Lanka, Nilgiri and Java tend to have this characteristic.

Nuwara Eliya: Growing region in the west of the Sri Lankan central massif well-known for its selected teas of very high quality "champagne grades". The name means "Above the clouds".

Off grades: English trade term for teas that fall outside the standard categories.

Oolong (Black Dragon): Fragrant semi-fermented tea, usually from Taiwan or China (Fuzhou, Amoy, Guangdong). A popular family tea often served at night and with meals. The best Oolongs produce a fine liquor of the colour of straw; cheaper ones tend to give a brown or red infusion. The United States and the Near Eastern countries are the chief importers of Oolong.

Orange: This category name has nothing to do with the fruit but is said to be derived from the Dutch royal house of that name and thus imply a "regal" quality.

Orange blossom: Mild China tea with the fragrance of orange blossom and oil.

Orange Pekoe (OP): Second grade teas on the British scale consisting of the finest young tips and curled leaves. Highland teas in this category are very fragrant. Orange Pekoe contains relatively little tannin.

Orchid tea: Black tea scented with orchids of the Aglaia odorata species. Often referred to as spiced tea.

Panfired: Term for an outdated process whereby fermented tea was baked in pans.

Panyong: Low quality China tea with lavender aroma.

Peach tea: Black or Oolong tea scented with peach blossoms and pieces of the fruit itself.

Pekko: The very young growth of the tea plant that is covered in a whitish bloom. The term comes from the word "pakko", meaning "white down". The final product, which tends not to be fermented, has a whitish or silver-grey colour.

Pekoe: Term from the British scale, denoting leaves slightly shorter and coarser than Orange Pekoe. The tips are picked with three leaves (instead of the usual two). The result is a plain tea producing a strong liquor.

Pekoe fannings (PF): Second smallest grade (only dust is smaller), usually used for tea-bags.

Pekoe Souchong (PS): Coarsest grade of tea, using the fourth to sixth leaf of the growth. Produces a thin liquor with high tannin content.

Peru: Produces relatively small quantities, mainly from the Cuzco region in the Quallabamba valley. The crop is harvested year round but is lowest in yield during the dry summer months. Most of the tea is Broken Orange Pekoe.

Pi Lo Chun: A fine China green leaf tea from Guangxi province that was first mentioned during the Sung dynasty as a present to the Emperor. The name was coined by the emperor K'ang-hsi who named three characteristics of the delicious tea: the silvery green of the young buds, the spiral form of the leaf and harvesting time during spring.

Pineapple tea: Tea scented with pineapple.

Pingsuey: Strong black China tea from the country's main growing region around the Yangtze Kiang. Strong, but not too bitter.

Plain: Used to describe a brew without freshness and aroma but with colour and strength. Can be caused by a plant being subject to too much rain during growth. This kind of tea usually goes into blends.

Plucking machine: High-quality tea can only be made from leaves harvested by hand. Tests with machines have been far from successful and are mainly used in Japan and the Soviet Union as a means of saving labour. The "Sakartwelo" machine, for instance, passes along the rows of bushes and removes all growth and leaves that extend beyond a certain limit.

Plucking: A good quality product comes from picking two leaves and a bud. Better teas use only one leaf and a bud, or sometimes merely the bud. More than two leaves and a bud, and the tea is described as a coarse plucking, as opposed to a fine plucking.

Point: Pleasantly dry and fresh Ceylon tea.

Pu erh beeng cha: Black China tea that promotes digestion and aids slimming. It originates from the southern Yunnan province where tea has been grown for over 1,700 years.

Rain tea: Tea harvested during the monsoon in northern India whose rapid growth often results in a thin brew that lacks any great fragrance.

Raw: Used to describe a tea with a bitter flavour.

Red: Tea with red leaves often signals a coarse pluck. It frequently fails to wither naturally and so is often put through the CTC process.

Rich: Describes a balanced, high-quality tea with all the best characteristics of colour and aroma.

Risheehat: Leading tea garden east of Darjeeling producing top quality leaf teas. The plantation was established by the German missionary family of Stölke who made an invaluable contribution to tea production in the area.

Ro: Square ceramic fireplace for use in the Japanese tea ceremony, let into the floor and surrounded by a wooden frame of mulberry or cedar wood (often lacquered).

Rose Congou: Chinese black tea scented with rose petals and rose oil.

Round: Describes above average teas producing full-flavoured brews.

Russian Tea: Highly aromatic, strong blend of Far Eastern and south Asian varieties. Caravan teas from China were formerly called Russian teas; the term implies a high quality.

Samovar: Charcoal-fired water heating apparatus widely used in Turkey, Iran and Russia. The flue is shrouded by a container that holds a strong tea essence, a quantity of which is tapped off, then topped up from the separate water boiler.

Scented Poochong: Lightly fermented China tea with aroma of jasmine blossoms.

Sechung Oolong: Semi-fermented China tea from the Amoy district, known for its peach-like aroma.

Seeyok: Tea garden in eastern Darjeeling on the Nepalese border, producing high-quality, second flush teas.

Self-drinking tea: A tea that is exclusively the product of one garden, not blended with tea of a different origin.

Sencha: Green Japanese variety, harvested in autumn. Has a faintly bitter aroma. Grows mainly in Shizuoka region.

Shadow tea: Variety produced in Japan having a particularly fine aroma, caused by its being grown in the shade of bamboo parasols which has a beneficial effect on the bushes.

Shizuoka: Japanese black tea from the Shizuoka region around Fujiyama, with a distinctive flavour.

Sichuan: Tea-growing region and province of China, producing mainly flowery black teas containing very little tannin.

Sikkim: Indian state in the eastern Himalayas where teas similar to Darjeeling varieties are grown, though in such small quantities that Sikkim tea rarely appears on the export market.

Silhead: Tea-growing region of northern India.

Smoky: Describes a brew with an unpleasant, burnt flavour that can be traced back to incorrect drying after fermentation.

Souchong: Large-leaved Chinese tea with smoky taste achieved by drying over a fire of highly resinous wood.

South America: Argentina, Brazil and Peru produce bulk teas that usually find their way into blends.

Soviet Union: Tea was first planted in what are now the southern republics of the USSR in 1884 on the slopes of the Caucasus between the Black Sea and Caspian Sea. As a result, caravan tea transported overland from the Far East is now of little significance.

Sow Mee (Eyebrows of long life; also Sho May or Soo May): Green China tea produced in Guangdong province, once traditionally served in the open air in spring. The Buddhist legend of Bodhidarma tells of the holy man's displeasure at his constant drowsiness causing him to cut off his eyebrows or eyelids, which he then threw to the ground, and which sprang to life as the first tea bushes.

Spring tea: The first crop in areas where harvesting does not take place all year round. Generally lighter and more flowery than the later crop.

Stalks: Careless picking results in stalks finding their way into the final product.

Steinthal: A small garden in Darjeeling established in the 19th century by Stoelke, the German missionary. Produces high quality leaf teas.

Strainer cup: Traditional design of Chinese tea cup.

The lid is positioned during drinking so as to catch the leaves, allowing the tea to be sucked through an opening.

Sui Seng (water nymph, also Shui sen, Shuy seen or Suy sien): Green China tea from Guangdong province. A pleasant, light refreshing tea very suitable for drinking in the late morning.

Sukiya: The room in which the Japanese tea ceremony takes place.

Su-lan: Chinese blend of black tea and oolong, scented with su-ho-hsiang blossom (a tree similar to the plane tree).

Sun-Moon: Black tea from the central highlands of Taiwan named after the lake on whose shores it flourishes.

Sunny Islands: Black tea scented with peach, mango and lemon.

Sutton: Nilgiri tea with tangy aroma.

Sweet Lemon: Mild China tea scented with lemon oil.

Taiwan: This island off the coast of China, also known as Formosa or the Republic of China, mostly produces inexpensive teas for export to the United States and Japan, including oolong, black and green varieties. The best of these are grown in the central highlands (see Sun-Moon).

Tannin: Important ingredient in tea. Buds and tips of the tea-bush contain tannin in lighter concentration than the leaves. During fermentation a great deal of the tannin is oxidized. Green teas thus contain larger amounts of tannin than black teas. It has a soothing effect on the membranes of the stomach and intestine.

Tarry Lapsang Souchong: Unblended smoked tea from China or Taiwan.

Tea blender: A tea-taster whose job it is to blend teas.

Tea-garden: A tea plantation of any size, even those large enough to have their own processing facilities and transport. The term has also been applied to restaurants serving tea laid out in the form of a garden.

Tea-houses: Establishments in China and Japan similar to European cafs. During the Baroque era, the vogue for anything Chinese caused many European princes and kings to incorporate tea-houses into their parks and gardens. The tea-room in the pagoda at Nymphenburg in Munich, and Frederick the Great's Chinese tea house at Sanssouci are notable examples of this cultural exchange.

Tea races: Races between tea clippers carrying their cargoes from the Far East to Britain.

Tea-shop: Shops (usually in Britain) where tea is sold in packets but which also serve tea to thirsty customers. They still exist, although they are becoming rarer.

Tea-taster: Professional employed by tea producers and merchants who grades teas according to their quality and often prepares blends on the basis of the results.

Tea-time: Traditional British break, not to be missed even in the direst circumstances. Cakes or a snack are often taken at the same time. The custom has often been condemned as a danger to trade and industry; a certain Lord Chancellor once demanded that a law be introduced to limit the taking of tea to "higher levels of society".

Tee Goon Yum (The iron goddess of compassion, also known as Iron Kwan Yin, Tit Koon Yum or Tweet Gwoon Yum): Black China tea from Fujian and Amoy. Thick and full-flavoured with an exquisite fragrance. Drunk in small quantities, like a good cognac.

Teenkai: Chinese region producing extremely fine green tea.

Teesta Valley: Well-known garden in eastern Darjeeling that overlooks Bhutan and China. Largely given over to production of leaf teas from China plants.

Theine: Stimulant in tea, identical to caffeine in coffee. Its chemical name is trimethyloxypurin. The substance promotes concentration and improves reactions. The compound is released immediately tea is brewed, and is therefore at its freshest after only 2 1/2/ to 3 1/2 minutes. After that time, tannin and other substances are released which have a soothing effect on the stomach and intestines.

Teoke: Wooden water-container used at beginning of Japanese tea ceremony to rinse the hands. A hollowed-out stone (chozubachi) is often used for the same purpose. The containers are complemented by a ladle of cypress or cedar wood, called a hishaku.

Terai: Region of northern India, at the foot of the mountains bordering on Darjeeling. Terai tea is generally no match for Darjeeling but the two are often blended.

Thick: Describes an infusion containing a high percentage of dissolved solids.

Thin: Describes an infusion that is pale and watery.

Tibet: Country annexed by China, to the west of the People's Republic, and a heavy consumer of tea. Tibetans prefer brick tea, grated and boiled, often with yak butter.

Tin kuan yin: Semi-fermented China tea producing a mild infusion; another name for Sechung Oolong.

Tip: Protective outer leaf of the bud, covered in tiny hairs; can be recognized in a black tea by its golden-yellow colouring. Tippy teas contain a high proportion of tips.

Tippy Golden Flowery Orange Pekoe (TGFOP): Second grade of leaf tea on the Indian scale.

Tired: Describes a very old tea, often incorrectly packed or stored. Sometimes produced by old, exhausted bushes.

Turkey: Tea has been grown in eastern Anatolia since 1924. Turkish tea is usually black, and produces a thin infusion. Only small quantities are exported.

Tukdah: First-class tea garden in north eastern Darjeeling, producing mainly leaf teas.

Tukvar: Large tea-garden in Darjeeling, known for its receptiveness to technical innovation. Mechanisation on this plantation began as early as 1872.

Tungsha: Chinese garden on the island of Hainan in the Gulf of Tonkin. First set up as a research project to inves-tigate ways of adapting small Chinese gardens to modern techniques.

Uji: Japanese town in the centre of a region known for production of first-class teas.

Uneven: Describes a carelessly processed tea, whose leaves are of different grades for instance, or inconsistently rolled. The result is a poor-quality tea.

Uva: Tea district on the eastern slopes of the Sri Lankan massif, between 4,000 and 6,000 feet above sea level. Fine-flavoured and highly aromatic varieties grow here, the best of which are picked in the summer, although harvesting goes on the whole year round.

Vanilla tea: Tea scented with vanilla from Madagascar.

Vietnam: Tea-planting was first recorded here in 1825 but has suffered badly from the ravages of war this century. It is now slowly recovering. Bulk teas are the chief output which are usually later blended with African varieties.

Viridis: Description which was once used for all green China tea.

White tea: Unfermented China tea consisting exclusively of buds with a white bloom. The leaves are dried individually in the open air. Also known as white downy tea. Produces a delicately flavoured but nevertheless aromatic infusion.

Withering: As harvested leaves shrivel up they lose a certain amount of their moisture content; withering is an important part of the production process.

Woody: Used to describe a tea, usually from an autumn harvest, that tastes of hay or grass; also known as wild woody.

Wun mo (*Cloud of Mist*): A famous green China tea from Guangxi province with an exquisite aroma that is usually drunk only in very small quantities, like a liqueur. Because it favours high altitudes which humans had difficulty reaching, it is said that apes were trained in ancient times to gather the leaves and bring them back to the valleys, which explains the other name sometimes given to the tea, Monkey Tea.

Yunnan: Mountainous province of southern China bordering on Laos and Burma. It produces teas which are mild with a faintly smoky flavour. One property of Yunnan teas, according to clinical tests, is that they lower the blood cholesterol level.

Yunnan-Darjeeling: Currently popular blend of strong Yunnans and fruity Darjeelings; makes an interesting breakfast tea.

The Recipes by Type

Unless otherwise stated, quantities are for four servings.

Cakes

Recipes in Alphabetical Order

Photo Sources

Acaluso International/China Features: 6, 10/11 (2), 65
Acaluso International/The Bettmann Archive: 28/29 r.
Anthony/Hoffmann-Burchardi: 49
Bildarchiv Preußischer Kulturbesitz: 13 (Shigemasa and Shunshô), 28 (2), 41
Bilderberg/Drexel: 54 t., 55 t.r., 56 (2)
Bilderberg/Francke: 48/49 l.
Bilderberg/Grames: 14/15 r., 17, 19, 38/39
Rosmarie Bosch-Burkhardt: 61, 62, 73
Das Deutsche Teebüro: 2, 33, 47
Porcelain Manufacture Gshelj: 71
Hetjens-Museum: 68
IFA/Aberham: 8
IFA/Kneuer: 5
IFA/WPS: 53
Jürgens: 67
Archiv Paul Schrader & Co.: 20/21, 22, 24/25,
50/51, 54 b., 55 t.l. and b., 59, 68/69 r.
Kurt Schröder and Albrecht von Tucher: 26
Schuster/Scholz: 14
Sirius Bildarchiv/Döbbelin: 63, 70/71 l., 74, 75, 77, 78–177
Sirius Bildarchiv/Wood: 45
Teehandelskontor Bremen: 34

SPECIALITY COOKBOOKS

The following have already been published in the same format.
Also available in English: "Dine around the world" and "Drinks".

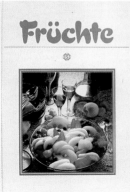

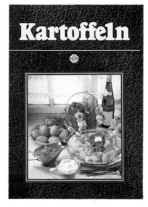